THE
SOLOMON
SECRET

7 Principles of Financial Success
from King Solomon,
History's Wealthiest Man

BRUCE FLEET
with ALTON GANSKY

JEREMY P. TARCHER/PENGUIN
a member of Penguin Group (USA) Inc.
New York

JEREMY P. TARCHER/PENGUIN
Published by the Penguin Group
Penguin Group (USA) Inc., 375 Hudson Street, New York,
New York 10014, USA • Penguin Group (Canada), 90 Eglinton Avenue East,
Suite 700, Toronto, Ontario M4P 2Y3, Canada (a division of Pearson Penguin Canada Inc.) •
Penguin Books Ltd, 80 Strand, London WC2R 0RL, England • Penguin Ireland,
25 St Stephen's Green, Dublin 2, Ireland (a division of Penguin Books Ltd) •
Penguin Group (Australia), 250 Camberwell Road, Camberwell, Victoria 3124,
Australia (a division of Pearson Australia Group Pty Ltd) • Penguin Books
India Pvt Ltd, 11 Community Centre, Panchsheel Park, New Delhi–110 017, India •
Penguin Group (NZ), 67 Apollo Drive, Rosedale, North Shore 0632, New Zealand
(a division of Pearson New Zealand Ltd) • Penguin Books (South Africa) (Pty) Ltd,
24 Sturdee Avenue, Rosebank, Johannesburg 2196, South Africa

Penguin Books Ltd, Registered Offices: 80 Strand, London WC2R 0RL, England

All Bible quotations unless otherwise noted are from the New International Version.

Scripture taken from the HOLY BIBLE, NEW INTERNATIONAL VERSION®
Copyright © 1973, 1978, 1984 International Bible Society. Used by permission of
Zondervan. All rights reserved.

The "NIV" and "New International Version" trademarks are registered in the United States Patent and Trademark
Office by International Bible Society. Use of either trademark requires the permission of International Bible Society.

Scripture taken from the NEW AMERICAN STANDARD BIBLE®
Copyright © 1960, 1962, 1963, 1968, 1971, 1972, 1973, 1975, 1977, 1995 by the
Lockman Foundation. Used by permission.

The author gratefully acknowledges permission to quote lyrics from "Loose Ends," words and music by
Dan Fogelberg. © 1977 (Renewed 2005) EMI April Music Inc. and Hickory Grove Music. All rights controlled and
administered by EMI April Music Inc. All rights reserved. International copyright secured. Used by permission.

Most Tarcher/Penguin books are available at special quantity discounts for bulk purchase for sales promotions,
premiums, fund-raising, and educational needs. Special books or book excerpts also can be created
to fit specific needs. For details, write Penguin Group (USA) Inc. Special Markets, 375 Hudson Street,
New York, NY 10014.

The Library of Congress catalogued the hardcover edition as follows:

Fleet, Bruce.
The Solomon secret: 7 principles of financial success from King Solomon, history's wealthiest man / Bruce Fleet
with Alton Gansky.
p.   cm.
ISBN 978-1-58542-735-2
1. Finance, Personal.   I. Gansky, Alton.   II. Title.
HG179.F546   2009   2009017491
332.024—dc22

ISBN 978-1-58542-818-2 (paperback edition)

Printed in the United States of America
1   3   5   7   9   10   8   6   4   2

BOOK DESIGN BY NICOLE LAROCHE

This publication is designed to provide accurate and authoritative information in regard to the subject matter covered. It
is sold with the understanding that the publisher is not engaged in rendering legal, accounting, or other professional services.
If you require legal advice or other expert assistance, you should seek the services of a competent professional.

While the author has made every effort to provide accurate telephone numbers and Internet addresses at the time of
publication, neither the publisher nor the author assumes any responsibility for errors, or for changes that occur after
publication. Further, the publisher does not have any control over and does not assume any responsibility for author or
third-party websites or their content.

To Michelle and Matthew,
my wonderful wife and son,
for your never-ending belief and support

CONTENTS

INTRODUCTION

What if I could get you some time alone with Bill Gates, founder and CEO of Microsoft, the world's leading software company, or with Warren Buffett, the CEO of Berkshire Hathaway and arguably the finest investor of modern times—the two wealthiest men in the world. Would you be interested?

Would you treasure having these brilliant men teach you about your financial and investment decisions? Good as they are, these men can't hold a candle to the unique person about to give us advice.

I want to help you reach new levels of success in your financial life. That's what I do for a living, and this book is my effort to help as many people as possible. There are scores of financial investment books, but this one is unique. I will be bringing my years of investing experience to the table, but someone else is going to help us—a person who died centuries ago, but whose writings continue to impact lives today. He was a leader, builder, ruler, and financial genius.

Whether you believe in the persons and stories of the Bible or not, there is much we can learn from them. In this book we are going to explore some of King Solomon's teachings. Solomon is considered the wisest and richest man of all time. (Yes, even with his wealth adjusted for inflation, King Solomon would be the wealthiest man today, with wealth that would easily eclipse Gates's and Buffett's combined worth.)

Why Solomon? Why should we listen to a man who lived three thousand years ago? What can an ancient king teach us about contemporary financial matters? Believe it or not, he has a lot to say to us.

In the earliest days of his reign, Solomon, motivated by fear of his inadequacy—he was only twelve when he took the throne—asked God for a gift. He could have had anything; think what he could have asked for. Solomon could have requested the mightiest army, an army that would almost guarantee his power over any oppressor; he could have asked for riches beyond compare so that he could be confident of securing the finest government advisers available to make him look good. But what he sought instead was extraordinary at that time, and it is extraordinary in our day. It is what I hope you learn more than anything else from his teachings.

King Solomon asked for WISDOM. Not money or more power. He asked for the ability to make sound judgments and to know the difference between good and evil. (You can read the account in the Old Testament passages 1 Kings 3:9 and 2 Chronicles 1:10.)

I believe that God was so impressed with Solomon's simple yet intuitive request, He granted him not only wisdom but also more riches, wealth, and honor than anyone in history.

Solomon is the poster child for wisdom and wealth, and much of his thinking is written down. It's available to anyone. This book makes use of it.

You may be reading this book because you either want to be an investor or are already one of the ninety million investors in the United States today. For our purposes, "investor" means more than someone who buys stocks and bonds; it also means someone who acquires real estate and works on other ways of making money. As you will soon come to see, the principles contained here from Solomon are far-reaching and hold multiple applications we can use in all aspects of life. Read this book slowly. If a lesson seems too simple, read it again. Sometimes the most life-changing truth comes dressed in simplicity.

For instance, we can enter into a complex discussion of Sir Isaac Newton's mathematical description of gravity or we can "simply" believe it works and choose not to jump off the roof to test it. Albert Einstein, as well as other scientists, searched for the "simple" mathematical equation that explains the universe. Quantum physics is telling us about interconnectedness and . . . sorry, back to investing. The point is: A simple truth is still a powerful truth.

I have been professionally involved in the investment industry for more than twenty years. I have been a senior executive, a national trainer, and a highly requested lecturer on investment topics. During that time, I have seen just about every investment scheme, technique, and process available. Notice I didn't say every investment known. Wall Street continues to create investment products for you to buy. (I cover investment products and shenanigans in great detail in my first book, *Demystifying Wall Street.*)

Drawing from my investment knowledge and experience, I hope to bring Solomon's words to life and help you apply them to your investment situation. Not that King Solomon needs my help. Solomon lived long before the dawn of contemporary investments.

That's where I come in. Solomon will give us the big picture of what is important and wise, and I'll provide the day-to-day applications.

With each lesson from Solomon, I will attempt to give examples of how the information can be used as a benefit or how I have seen it misused by the foolish. We are going to cover some things that you would expect: goal setting and even a discussion of greed. We will also cover a few things you may not expect, like how generosity can help you grow your own wealth. This will not be a sermon—I promise.

As you will see, each chapter has two parts. First we will hear a little from Solomon, and then I'll bring a twenty-first-century application that you can use to further your investing knowledge.

So let's dig in. Let the words of Solomon marinate in your mind. Share these lessons with those you love, with those who are depending on your wisdom. By all means, discuss these lessons with those who help you manage your money.

It's time to get started, but first let's meet Solomon and his protégé.

ABIDAN

Abidan harbored two wishes. First, he wished to be anyplace but here. Second, he wished his knees weren't shaking. The walk from his home on the northeastern side of Jerusalem seemed to him far too short and his arrival far too early. A servant escorted him to the palace, then another led him into the massive building. Had it not been for the assigned attendants, Abidan would not have had the courage to travel from home to . . . to . . . here.

The servant at his side stood tall, proud, and confident, as if he had been born to the station he held. He moved with the kind of confidence that came from bravery. A quiet man, he had said only two words: "This way." The sight of the interior robbed Abidan of breath. Beneath his feet were massive, hand-cut stone slabs that formed the foundation. Seeming to hover above him were cedar beams and planks, and the walls were covered in wood panels carved by the finest craftsmen.

They passed through a cavernous room filled with three rows of fifteen stone columns each, cool and smooth to the touch. Scores of gold shields hung on the walls.

"Five hundred," the servant said.

"*Five hundred?*"

"*The number of gold shields on the wall. Every visitor asks. You were thinking of asking.*"

Abidan started to deny it, but thought it best not to lie to this man. "*What is this place?*"

"*The House of the Forest of Lebanon.*"

"*The columns make it look like a forest.*"

"*And so the name.*"

Abidan's heart trotted in his chest like a horse as he and the servant passed into another room. Here fine stone formed a wainscot a third of the way up the walls, and white plaster with paintings of plants and animals filled the space between the stone and the cedar ceiling soaring overhead. To one side rested a throne on a raised dais.

"*Is this . . . I mean, is this . . . ?*"

"*Yes,*" the servant said, "*it is the throne hall.*"

They passed through other large rooms and then outside to an enclosed courtyard filled with flowering plants, tall trees, and burbling fountains. A man, younger than Abidan's father and not yet elderly, stood with his face turned skyward. He wore a long robe, and his dark hair had begun to gray.

"*O King,*" the servant said, "*Abidan, son of Zerah, has arrived.*"

"*Thank you,*" the king said. "*You may go.*"

The servant was gone a moment later. That was when Abidan's knees began to shake. He started to speak, but words refused to come. His feet had grown roots, holding him in place.

"*Come to me, boy.*"

With his heart kicking like a donkey, Abidan forced his feet to move. With every step his sandals grew heavier. Still he crossed the courtyard and stood by the king's side. "*I . . .*" He choked. "*I . . . am here at your request, O King.*"

Solomon turned to face the boy. "*So I see. You are frightened?*"

"*Yes, O King.*"

"*How old are you?*" Solomon's voice was smooth and controlled.

"*I have reached my thirteenth year.*"

"*You are a man, then?*"

"*Yes . . . yes.*"

Solomon nodded. "*Do you know why you are here?*"

"*No, King. Your servant brought word of your desire to see me. That is all I know.*"

"*I see. And how is your father, Zerah?*"

"*He is well. The cold nights bother his joints.*" Abidan wondered why he added that.

"*It is the way of life. I have not seen him in many years.*"

Abidan struggled to believe his ears. "*You know my father?*"

"*Yes, I do. He gave me much good advice that helped me when I was a young king. Do you know much about advice?*"

"*No, King. I do not.*"

"*Long before your birth, I promised your father any favor he would ask. Of the many things he could have requested, he asked that I teach you.*"

"*Me?*"

"*He knew someday he would have a son, and he wanted the best for him. I am to be your tutor on a few matters.*"

"*I am not worthy of your time, O King.*" Abidan lowered his head.

"*We will see.*"

"*What am I to learn?*"

"*Did you see my palace?*"

Abidan nodded. "*Yes. It is the most beautiful thing I have ever seen . . . other than the Holy Temple, of course . . . which you built.*"

"*It took over seven years to build the Temple and thirteen years to build this palace. I have learned much in my years and God has given me great wisdom. I will share some of that with you.*"

"It is said, O King, that you know over three thousand proverbs and sayings."

"It is true, and I will share some with you, but you must promise to listen and heed my words. Will you do that?"

"Yes, O King."

"Then the lessons begin . . ."

I. THE SAYING

"Abidan."

"Yes, O King."

"Tell me the meaning of this proverb: 'Finish your outdoor work and get your fields ready; after that, build your house'" [Proverbs 24:27].

Abidan feared things would begin this way. It was bad enough standing next to the king in his private courtyard, but to be quizzed by the most powerful and wealthy man in the world made his stomach drop like an olive from a tree. "I do not know. I am not clever with such things. I am sorry if I disappoint you, O King."

"Not having an answer is no disgrace, son; not searching for an answer is. Listen as I repeat the proverb."

Solomon recited the words again and waited.

A bead of sweat ran down Abidan's spine. "Finish your outdoor work and get your fields ready; after that, build your house."

"That is good. Say it again."

Abidan repeated the proverb three more times.

"Now you have the words but you lack the meaning. Tell me what the saying teaches."

For a moment Abidan considered lying, but dealing falsely with the king would disgrace his father and certainly irritate his ruler. "It teaches that building a house is unimportant. It is hard work that matters most."

Solomon frowned. "This grand house that you have just seen, do you think it unimportant?"

"No, of course not, King. It is majestic, the best that any man has ever built."

"That is correct."

"I gave the wrong answer to your question."

This time Solomon smiled. "That is also correct. Try again."

Abidan chewed the words in his mind. A moment later it hit him. "The proverb teaches that if a man does not meet his immediate need, then he cannot meet his future needs."

"Correct!" Solomon slapped Abidan on the shoulder hard enough to send a lighting bolt of pain through the boy's body. "But there is more. Why fields first, house second?"

Again Abidan rehearsed the words. "If a man does not plant his fields, his family will have no food. A fancy house will be of no use to him."

"Zerah will be proud of you. You may tell him that you have pleased me."

"Thank you, King."

"There remains more to learn. Do you and your father farm?"

Abidan shook his head. "No, King, my father works in wood and teaches me the craft." Abidan was certain the king already knew this.

"So then, the proverb is useless to you?"

Solomon walked to a fountain, sat on a hand-carved stone bench, and motioned for Abidan to do the same.

Abidan suspected the answer was no. "Proverbs may have more than one meaning."

"Very good, Abidan. What meaning does the saying have for you?"

Each question dug deeper and taxed Abidan's mind more. "I . . . I am failing you, O King."

Solomon spoke softly. "No, Abidan, you have not failed me. You are here to learn. Wisdom comes to those who search for it, but not to those who wait for it. Do you understand?"

"I do."

"Then tell me what the saying means for you."

Abidan took a deep breath and let it out slowly. "If it is wise for a farmer to first plant his fields so that his family will have food and to do so before he builds his home, then . . . then . . . I should first . . . do the work today that will make for a good tomorrow."

Solomon's laughter was deep and echoed through the courtyard, setting doves to flight. "Yes, Abidan, wisdom has found you and you have found it."

The king leaned forward and dipped his finger in the water of the fountain. "Tell me, Abidan, how did this water come to be on my finger?"

"You placed your finger in the water."

"And how did the water come to be there?"

Abidan furrowed his brow. "I suppose someone carried the water to the fountain."

"And—"

"And they brought the water because the fountain had been built, and the fountain was built because the courtyard had been built, and the courtyard was built because the palace—"

"I think you have found the point of the spear, Abidan. The wise man does the first thing first, the second thing second, and so on."

"But how do I know what the first thing is?"

"You walked here today?"

"Yes, King."

"What was the first road you traveled?"

"The one in front of my house."

"A man and his work, his money, are the same. You start where you are, but you must also have a destination. A man works today, but his mind is on tomorrow."

"So, if I am to be wise I must think on tomorrow while working today."

Solomon closed his eyes and turned his face to the morning sun. "Does that sound simple to you, Abidan?"

"In some ways, King, but more than simple."

"The wisdom is indeed simple, but the practice it is hard." He lowered his face and stared at Abidan. "The wise man plans and continues to plan."

"I understand."

A polite cough came from behind them. Solomon and Abidan turned. The servant who'd led Abidan to the courtyard stood a short distance away but remained silent. Solomon nodded. "I must go. I will see you tomorrow. Give my kind thoughts to your father and mother."

"Tomorrow?"

Solomon stood. "A man does not come to wisdom in one day, Abidan."

CHAPTER 1

"THINK FIRST"

IN A NUTSHELL: The first step to success begins
with the words "I gotta plan."

Where there is no vision, the people are unrestrained.
— KING SOLOMON (PROVERBS 29:18; NASB)

I f you were building a house, chances are you wouldn't begin
purchasing the building materials before designing the plans.
Likewise, if you were driving from New York to Denver, you
would certainly find a map helpful.

Why, then, do so many investors explore investment programs
that may sound good, before having a detailed plan in place?

As a professional investment adviser, I have seen countless investors participate in programs that make no sense for their investment
portfolio. Let me give you an example: A retired investor has a need
for income-producing investments in order to supplement her Social
Security/pension income. A friend tells her about an investment that
has grown at double-digit rates for over ten years but pays no income; however, the future looks outstanding for the company.

Without knowing anything else about this woman, you understand how this investment, as good as it may be for someone else, doesn't fit her needs. Why? Because it's been established that the investor needs income to supplement what she's receiving from other sources.

> *Planning is bringing the future into the present so that you can do something about it now.*
>
> —ALAN LAKEIN,
> author of *How to Get Control of Your Time and Your Life*

There are many investment dangers lurking for the person searching for investments without having a clear and concise investment plan. I assure you that with sources like *Money* magazine, CNBC, friends, co-workers, TV commercials, and print advertisements you will come in contact with all sorts of investment possibilities that sound really good—but are they right for you? Do they fit your plans? Do they meet your needs?

The first lesson in wisdom from Solomon is consistent with what I have witnessed throughout my long investment career: You *must*—and I mean absolutely *must*—have a plan before you go into action.

PLAN TO PLAN

Most investors have multiple goals, because they have several stages and events in life for which they are planning. You may be preparing for a child's college education while at the same time planning your own retirement. Another person may be saving for a dream home while investing to accumulate money to start a new business, or write a book. (I'm living this last one.)

Understanding the "what" in our plan is a critical first step.

What you are investing for? *What* are you trying to accomplish? *What* goal do you have in mind? Yet the "what" is only the beginning.

Let's say you realize that there are a few different "whats" in your life. Which "what" should take priority? It's not always as simple as the child's college education will take place prior to your retirement, so you might as well start there. It's not that easy. You may need to start saving and investing for both goals at the same time. Yet, for most of us, there is a limit to how much money we can save.

That means something must take priority. Here is a personal opinion: I am a huge believer in living debt-free. Common knowledge tells us the three greatest stresses in life are financial, marital, and health. Financial stress many times leads to marital tension and can certainly cause health problems.

So if you need to prioritize, I would suggest the following as a general rule. Pay off any unsecured debt. That means credit cards, lines of credit, and the like. Most of these types of credit charge HUGE interest rates, some as high as 25 percent (I've seen some even higher). Pay them off, and most important, don't use them again. Period. By doing so you get a guaranteed rate of return equal to the amount of interest you were paying. You will most likely never find quality investments that pay that rate of return.

THE BEST WAY UP IS TO PAY DOWN

Next, work to pay down, or pay off, your mortgage. There is no feeling like living in a home that has a huge equity balance. I remember the first time I walked into my home after writing a check for the final mortgage payment. Wow! It was like coming home for the first time. I sat in my reading chair (of course, this chair is off-limits to everyone in the house other than me and my cat, although the dogs break the rule when I'm not home) and relished the thought that this house was mine. No one could take it away from me. What an awesome feeling.

I know this may not seem like a big deal, but I can't emphasize how important and freeing it is. Other financial advisers often counsel against paying off a mortgage. After all, your mortgage provides a huge tax deduction and you are using other people's money. But there is more to it than that. By paying off your mortgage you not only realize a financial freedom, but also have the satisfaction of knowing that you, not the bank, own your home. I understand the logic of mortgages, but I can't tell you how many times, as an investment adviser, I helped a couple pay off their mortgage and later received a letter or call from the wife thanking me for encouraging them to do so. Generally, women are more concerned with financial security than with the growth of an investment portfolio. It's a generalization, I know, but my experience tells me it's true. Trust me, debt-free living is liberating to mind and heart.

SAVE IT!

Finally, save like crazy for your retirement. Max out your company-sponsored retirement plan. If your company puts money in the plan, treat it as a gift—but that's no substitute for your personal contribution. I will say it again because it's so important: Fund your retirement to the max. Pretax retirement saving is one of the most powerful ways to save and invest.

I would go so far as to say you have no business starting an additional investment program until you have reached the maximum retirement savings allowed by law. Saving money on a pretax basis (the money comes out of your pay before taxes) and allowing it to grow on a tax-deferred basis is really powerful.

You may notice that I have yet to suggest college savings. I know putting little Judy and Johnny through college is an important part of your overall life strategy, but there are two points I would like you to con-

> *Let our advance worrying become advance thinking and planning.*
>
> —SIR WINSTON CHURCHILL, author and two-time prime minister of the United Kingdom

sider. First, if you focus your saving and investing efforts on college education but not retirement savings, there may come a time when little Judy and Johnny may have to support you. Not good.

Second, and more realistically, the federal and state governments provide access to grants, scholarships, and low-cost subsidized loans for higher education. I'm simply saying that there is no excuse for any American not to attend college these days. If you are taking care of your other financial needs responsibly, and have additional discretionary income, then by all means save for college.

The Apostle Paul said, "If anyone does not provide for his relatives, and especially for his immediate family, he has denied the faith and is worse than an unbeliever" (1 Timothy 5:8).

Those may seem like harsh words. You may also think that my thoughts on college saving are inconsistent with Scripture. I would disagree and add that sometimes placing financial responsibility on an adult child *is* providing for family. I would love everyone to fund their children's higher education, but I also know that not everyone can.

Let's move on . . .

THE FINANCIAL STOPWATCH

After creating a solid and realistic list of the things you are saving and investing for, you should attach a time frame to each goal. For instance, if you are thirty-five years old now and would like to retire at sixty, the time frame is twenty-five years. Twenty-five years is a long time. After all, it's a quarter of a century, right? Don't be fooled. It may seem like you have plenty of time and can put this off for a while. The issue to be considered is the exceptionally large dollar amount that needs to be accumulated in order to accomplish the task.

Assume for a moment that you need $65,000 per year from your retirement savings to replace your current income. Also assume that your current income is $80,000 per year and you expect to receive $15,000 from Social Security or another pension plan. You would need to accumulate $928,571 in principal and generate a 7 percent rate of return to receive the $65,000 needed. Twenty-five years may not seem that long a time when you think of it that way.

Do this type of calculation for each of your goals. Make certain that each goal is realistic and attainable. If you come to see that a goal of yours is completely unrealistic, rethink your strategy. The point here is to have a vision. Build a financial road map, if you will. Be specific.

Look at how much we have covered, and we have yet to talk about investing specifics. That will come a bit later. I want you to

THE SOLOMON SECRET | 15

realize how powerful Solomon's words are and how clearly they relate to today's times. As a professional in the field who has witnessed countless investors both succeed and fail, I can assure you that without a clear and concise plan, you will fail. But with a good plan, you will succeed.

Your investment plan is so important that I intentionally placed it first in the book. I think Solomon would have agreed.

Younger readers may be thinking, "I live paycheck to paycheck and I can't save right now, but I will when I start making more money." Take it from someone who has been on every part of the earnings spectrum. The time to start is now . . . or sooner.

> *Make no little plans; they have no magic to stir men's blood and probably will themselves not be realized. Make big plans; aim high in hope and work, remembering that a noble, logical diagram once recorded will not die.*
>
> —ATTRIBUTED TO
> DANIEL H. BURNHAM,
> architect and urban planner

I can promise you that when you start making more money, you will have a larger house, a more expensive car, or a more lavish lifestyle. It's a circular trap. We will talk more on this later, but you need to understand that saving must start now.

Early in my own work history, I was newly married and earning just enough to get us by. One day my lovely bride said she needed money to go to the grocery store to get the essentials—milk, eggs, and the like. I told her that she would need to wait until Friday, when I got paid. That went over like a lead balloon. She said, in a firm tone, "Why do you save so much for your retirement when we need the money now?"

It would have been very easy to forgo my savings plan so we would have more take-home pay. We survived. Years later I can assure you my wife is happy that I saved so aggressively. When times got tough later on (as when I decided to become a writer), we had plenty of money saved to get us through.

The bottom line is, save now, even if it is just a little. The one thing you have going for you is time, so take advantage of it. Albert Einstein once said that compounding interest is the "eighth wonder of the world."

Older readers may feel discouraged that so much time has passed and they are "behind the eight ball." Well, that's true in part; yet, still no excuse for not starting. There are federal rules on retirement saving that allow you to save more. They are called the "make up" provisions.

Wealth creation is a two-sided coin: Saving and investing. At the start we are talking about saving because it is truly the more important of the two. Think of it this way: If you don't save, you will have nothing to invest.

Saving and planning will place you way ahead of the pack and give you a much higher chance at success. We've all heard of people who worked the same job for thirty-plus years, never earning a large salary, only to find at retirement that they had a wonderful, seven-figure nest egg. They were good, steady savers.

Saving is a bit like dieting. Stay with me on this one.

Nobody likes to diet. Some people, like me, always have to diet even to maintain a constant weight. I have, in my genetic code, what we dieters like to call "the fat gene." (If we were in church I would certainly get an amen on that one.) Think about it. You have to give up things that you really like. Sometimes, like at night, it is uncomfortable. We substitute immediate gratification for a future goal.

Yet, if we tell the truth and stop whining about it, taking control does help us feel empowered. When we see those pounds dropping, we give ourselves a mental high-five. And when we hit our target weight, catch a glimpse of our new bod in the mirror, we say, "It was worth it."

Isn't that like saving? I would like you to start thinking of it that way. Be empowered, take control, celebrate the small steps, and work toward a goal. I can assure you, in the end you will say, "It was worth it."

> **JUST FOR FUN . . .**
>
> *Money frees you from doing things you dislike. Since I dislike doing nearly everything, money is handy.*
>
> —GROUCHO MARX, entertainer

Questions to Ask Yourself

1. What do I really want in life? Take time to give this some serious thought.
2. What are the priorities in my life? What matters most to me?
3. How well does my current financial situation fit with these priorities? Be honest with yourself, even if it's painful.
4. What needs to change? Be specific.
5. What should my first few steps on this new journey be?

Wisdom's To-Do List

1. List specific goals (the "whats"). Take the time to write them down so you can review them frequently.
2. Visualize your life as if those goals have been obtained.

3. Once you are comfortable with those goals, set a time-table to achieve each one. Adjust the table as necessary. Remember, life is fluid.

4. Chose a debt to pay off. Once the debt is gone, take the money you were previously paying and *add* it to a payment you're making on another bill. When that bill is gone, take the combined payments and add it to the payment being made on another debt.

5. Look for ways to save. Small amounts add up quickly.

6. Review your goals at least once a week.

ANCIENT ADVICE

1 TIMOTHY 5:8—If anyone does not provide for his relatives, and especially for his immediate family, he has denied the faith and is worse than an unbeliever.

PROVERBS 29:18—Where there is no revelation [vision], the people cast off restraint; but blessed is he who keeps the law.

II. THE WALL

When Abidan arrived at the palace the same servant greeted him. Again he was led through massive paneled rooms. Every step caused his heart to beat a little faster. The king had been gracious to him last time, so he felt less fearful but no more confident.

As they reached the throne room, the servant stopped. Abidan did the same. The day before, the room had been empty, but now the king sat on the throne, stroking his beard. Moments later, he spoke, but so softly that Abidan couldn't hear. The men before the king nodded.

"What happens here?" Abidan asked.

"The king often serves as judge. These men have a dispute. The king will give the final word. His wisdom is known everywhere."

"And he shares that wisdom with others?"

"It wouldn't be wisdom if he did not. He shares it with you. He shares it where it is needed."

The men left and the servant escorted Abidan into the throne room. Light poured through windows near the high ceiling, splashing on the walls. Solomon stood and motioned for Abidan to approach.

"It is good to see you again, Abidan. Did you have a good night?"

"I thought about all you taught me yesterday."

"Does it seem right to you?"

"It does, O King."

Solomon seemed pleased. "Walk with me." He descended the steps that led from the elevated throne to the stone floor. "I wish to show you something."

Abidan walked to the side and a step behind his king as Solomon led him through the palace, into the courtyard where they'd met the day before, and around the back of the building. A short distance away, six workmen labored on a garden wall.

"What do you see?" Solomon asked.

"Workmen," Abidan said, then thought he should be more specific. "Stonemasons."

"What are they doing?"

"Working, O King."

Solomon sighed. "Look closer."

Abidan studied the men for a moment. "They're removing stones from the wall."

"Yes."

"I do not understand, King. The wall looks in good condition and new."

"It is new," Solomon said. "It was finished only ten days ago."

"Then why destroy what has already been built?"

"It was built well and strong, but not according to plan. The man I hired to do the work had to travel to Galilee while his men continued to build the wall. He left specific instruction on how it should be built and the curve it should take. When he returned from the north country, the wall was finished but not to his specifications."

"So you have made him do the work again."

"No. I gave no such command."

Abidan looked at Solomon. "But King, here he is with his men, working."

"He came to me the day he returned, apologized, and asked my permission to remove the improper portion of the wall and rebuild it as it should be. Of course, I said yes."

"He offered to fix his mistake?"

"He took responsibility for his work. He offered to make it right."

"Did he blame his men?"

Solomon shook his head. "No, Abidan, he didn't. He said the fault was his."

"But King, he was many miles away."

"Exactly. What does that teach you?"

"To hire wisely."

Solomon laughed. "Yes, that is wise, but not today's lesson. Try again."

"The stonemason trusted his men to do the work correctly but they did not, so . . ." Abidan trailed off in thought. "He did not blame his men but blamed himself."

"Good. Keep going."

"I don't know."

"I believe you do. What are the builder and his men doing now?"

"Tearing down and rebuilding the wall."

"Why?"

"Because it was done wrong . . . and the builder believes it is his responsibility to do what he said he would."

"Very good, Abidan. The word 'responsibility' is the key. The builder is one of my favorites. He does exceptional work, not because I demand it, but because he takes responsibility for his business."

"So if I am to be wise, I must not turn my back on my responsibility for my . . . work?"

"And decisions, and finances, and family, and everything else."

"I see."

Solomon closed his eyes and recited, *"The plans of the diligent lead to profit as surely as haste leads to poverty."*

"Another proverb."

"Yes. What does it mean?"

"Hard work leads to wealth."

"No, true as that is. But I did not mention hard work." Solomon repeated the proverb.

"You said 'diligent.'"

"A wise man is a diligent man. He not only works hard, but he works correctly, he works with a plan, he knows what the end looks like. Our builder knew what the wall should be. That was his goal, but the men he left in charge failed to make his vision come true, so he is seeing to it himself. What is the lesson in that?"

"Not to trust others . . ." Abidan saw the frown forming at the king's mouth. *"To . . . have a goal and work toward it."*

"Yes. And who is responsible for that goal?"

"The builder."

"And in your life?"

It became clear. *"I am responsible. To be wise and to build wealth, I must be diligent—working hard but with a clear purpose. I am responsible for what I dream, what I do."*

"You grow in wisdom, Abidan, but be careful. You must see beyond the money. Whoever loves money never has enough; whoever loves wealth is never satisfied with his income."

"I think I understand. The stonemason does this extra work not because of the money but because he is responsible for the way the wall looks and where it is built."

"The builder believes he is losing money, which he is for now. I shall

reward his diligence. Now, Abidan, tell me in one line what you have learned."

"I alone am responsible for my dreams, my money, and my work. To be wise, I must be diligent in all those things."

"That is two lines, Abidan, but acceptable." Solomon turned and started back to the palace. "I must return and judge a grievance between two women."

CHAPTER 2

"THE SHEKEL STOPS HERE"

IN A NUTSHELL: Gird up thy financial trousers.
Your money is your responsibility.

You cannot escape the responsibility of tomorrow by evading it today.

—ABRAHAM LINCOLN

I t's *your* money.

It's *your* financial future.

And it's *your* responsibility.

That could easily be the end of this chapter. Yet, I do have a few thoughts on this topic.

I can't count the times I have seen investors, both in my practice, as well as throughout the industry, who seem to think it "just fine" to turn over full responsibility for their financial future to a "professional" whom they know little about. That is a great deal of power to surrender to someone else.

In a later chapter we will think through the appropriate use of professionals. Please do not find this contradictory. The only way a professional relationship works is if both parties are constantly reminded that the money and the future belong to you.

Previously we discussed the "what" and "when" of your investment plan. Hopefully, you have started to compile a list of the "what" items and assigned a time frame target for each of these items. Now we are going to focus on the "why" you are saving and investing.

Over the last twenty years, I have asked thousands of investors why they invest. The answers are always interesting.

"To make extra money."

"To keep pace with inflation."

"To become wealthy."

Believe it or not, these are fairly lousy answers. Yet when I compile all of the answers I have heard over the years and condense them down to what I believe to be the root concept, I arrive at this: People save and invest to provide *financial freedom* for themselves and their families.

Isn't that a wonderful term? *Financial freedom.* I can't imagine anyone not wanting to be free from the worry of money matters. When someone is financially free, then they are "life-free." By that I mean they can experience life with much less concern and pressure.

The question then begs to be asked, What is financial freedom? No doubt different people will give different answers; nevertheless, I have found significant commonality among most individuals.

Consider a few illustrations. "I want to be certain that my family has enough money to always take care of ourselves." Or, "I never want to be a financial burden on my children." Or, "I want to be sure that my children are taken care of and my wife and I can have a comfortable retirement."

My mom used to live in Hollywood Beach, Florida. In warm-weather areas of the country, it is not uncommon to see street-people who carry their possessions around in a shopping cart full of bags. When my mother and I would talk about financial free-dom, she would always say, "I just don't want to be a bag lady."

I'm not trying to be melodramatic—I am trying to impress upon you the importance of your financial future. This is not something you simply place on the shoulders of another and say, "I don't understand invest-ing, so you take care of it." I will repeat, and probably not for the last time: It's *your* money, *your* financial future, and *your* responsibility.

> *We all have dreams. But in order to make dreams into reality, it takes an awful lot of determina-tion, dedication, self-discipline, and effort.*
>
> —JESSE OWENS,
> winner of four
> Olympic gold medals

LIFE, LIBERTY, AND A LESS STRESSFUL LIFE

Another aspect of financial freedom could be liberty from financial stress. Unless you were born wealthy, you have probably experi-enced times of monetary strain. It is never fun to have creditors calling the house during dinnertime, demand letters constantly in the mail, arguments between spouses or parents and children. Fi-nancial stress often leads to marital and family problems, and can certainly impact your health.

Listen to Solomon: "The plans of the diligent lead to profit as surely as haste leads to poverty" (Proverbs 21:5).

When Solomon wrote that proverb, he knew what he was talking about.

So what is Solomon saying? In a nutshell: "Diligence leads to profit." Do you find that to be true in other areas of your life? If you desire to excel in a sport, you train with diligence and effort. If you wanted to do well in college, you found the harder you worked, the better you understood the subject matter, and that led to better grades. Marriage takes work. Relationships of all kinds take work. Excelling in your job requires work. This isn't high philosophy; it's a fact of life.

Are you willing to put forth the work, the diligence required to achieve financial freedom? If so, then there's a very good chance you will succeed. Now here's some good news: You won't have to go it alone. We will discuss working with professionals later, but for now, I simply want you to accept responsibility for your financial future.

Psychology teaches us the principle: "You achieve what you focus on." Others state it a bit differently, saying, "What you measure, you attain." Both of these statements have been proven over the last few decades.

While watching the winter Olympics I noticed ski jumpers waiting their turn to barrel down a long ramp covered in snow and ice to launch themselves into the air, hoping to fly farther than their competitors. As I watched the athletes, I noticed they spent their waiting time with eyes closed and moving their bodies an inch here and an inch there. They were imagining, seeing in their minds, what it was they were about to do. The more events I watched, the more I noticed competitors doing this. It was especially visible with luge and bobsled riders, who imagined each turn before they started their downhill trek. For them, to imagine it was the same as doing it.

Many athletes and coaches consider visualization of the activity and of the desired goal a critical part of training. Some coaches believe this aspect of the process is even more important than the physical training.

Writing down your financial goals, the "whats" on your list, and attaching a specific time frame to achieve the objectives—your personal definition of financial freedom—compose the visualization process. There is even a greater impact on your imagination if you build a picture-book representation of your life goals.

Let's say one of your goals is a beachfront house where you hope to spend your retirement. Find a picture of an ideal representation of this goal and paste it in your book. If your dream is funding a child's college education, then get a picture of a smiling college grad and put it in the book. Don't laugh, this works.

Now write a description on the back of each picture, or on the opposite page, detailing how it would *feel* to achieve these things. How would these achievements change your life? Would these things offer you a sense of peace?

This is a very individual process, though if you're married, it can and should be done as a couple. Having both spouses on the same pathway creates an accountability partner, a support person, and a degree of shared responsibility.

A long time ago, I created a book just like the one I've described. I had a picture of a custom-built home, with large, heavy doors. There was a photo of a beautiful airplane glimmering in the sun. Another image was of an expensive, fast, sporty convertible.

I would look through this picture book every morning before I went to work and every evening before bed. A few years later, I was driving my convertible en route to the local airport, where I had recently learned to fly, and then on to my custom-built home for dinner.

I was young and my goals were self-centered, but still the technique worked and it was certainly a lot of fun.

> Success on any major scale requires you to accept responsibility. . . . In the final analysis, the one quality that all successful people have . . . is the ability to take on responsibility.
>
> —MICHAEL KORDA, author and editor

As we age, our goals change. Now I have a goal of giving a lot of money away. This certainly would not have been in my first dream book. All that is to say that your goals will evolve. You must allow for change as you age. Just know that the process works.

As you may have guessed, I have attempted to involve your senses in the process. Writing down a goal is powerful to one person, while viewing a picture is more useful to another. The best thing is to be specific in a way that best suits your personality.

"Do you see a man skilled in his work? He will serve before kings; he will not serve before obscure men" (Proverbs 22:29).

Let's say you desire to become skilled at something. What would you do? You would probably read books on the subject. You might watch instructional videos. You would certainly utilize the Internet. Many local colleges and universities offer classes you can take to help you learn the skills required. The more important the subject is to you, the more effort you will apply in learning it. So what are we talking about? Just your *entire* financial future. Is that worth learning a few new skills? Of course it is. The more you see the importance of the topic, the greater your desire to master it will become.

The greatest challenge in learning about investments is choosing your teacher. Unfortunately, there are a lot of scam artists who offer instruction as bait to draw you into their investment program. I offer this general rule: Beware the teacher who has a product to sell or newsletter subscription to buy. Warren Buffett is one of the two richest men in the world and one of the greatest investors of all time. Mr. Buffett has nothing to sell you. He would be a good example of a quality teacher. (A recommended list of reading materials is noted in the appendix.)

There is no one source of quality investment information. You can learn from all of them as long as you keep in mind their motivation. For instance, CNBC business channel has some good insight on the investment markets as well as individual companies. Keep in mind that CNBC has an enormous amount of airtime to fill. Also remember that any television or print media must sell advertising in order to keep the lights on. So even CNBC has a motive for providing news and commentary.

Again, this doesn't mean you can't learn from them as long as you remind yourself there is no holy grail of investment advice. I have known people who keep the financial news channel on the entire day. This is ridiculous on numerous fronts, not the least of which is that there is more to life than watching a business channel.

WHAT OWNS WHO HERE?

This leads me to another point of this chapter, in case you missed it. To take responsibility and learn more about your finances is good; to have money and investment planning engulf your entire life is foolishness.

Solomon wrote, "Whoever loves money never has enough; whoever loves wealth is never satisfied with his income" (Ecclesiastes 5:10).

> *Make money your god and it will plague you like the devil.*
>
> —HENRY FIELDING,
> eighteenth-century
> novelist and dramatist

Solomon is teaching us to set life goals, to take care of our family and our future, but not to allow money to consume us. In other words, money is not the root of all evil, but the *love* of money can cause serious problems.

Comedian and actor Robin Williams tells of a young boy who asked his father where the quarter of a million dollars was that his father had saved. Startled, the father said, "What in the world are you talking about?" The boy responded that his teacher had taught in class that if a person saved $2,000 per year (or $167 a month) in a retirement account earning 8 percent, he or she would have amassed over $250,000 in only thirty years. So the little boy, now understanding how easy it was to save, wanted to know where the money was.

The morals of the story are: (1) Saving and compounding work; (2) The math is easy; and (3) It's the discipline to save that is the hard part.

Discipline. Isn't that always the hard part? Anything in life that is worth achieving seems to require discipline. The first thing I tell clients is, "I can help you make good investments, but I can't help you save. That is your job."

If discipline is a vehicle used to drive you toward the attainment of a financial objective, then a clear vision, consisting of well-defined goals and objectives, is the fuel. The discipline to save is a form of delayed gratification. Once again, the question should be, Is it worth it?

I ask you to think about your own parents. Did they work hard during their lives, raising children, attending to the needs of the home, working their jobs? For many people I speak with, the answer to these questions is a resounding yes. When I follow up with a question that involves the retirement experience of their parents, many tell me that their parents deserved more.

For many, looking at their parents is like peeking into their own future. If your parents are enjoying a wonderful retirement, filled with the financial security to enjoy life, family, travel, or whatever it is that they most take pleasure in, then learn what they did to achieve this outcome.

The opposite of this scenario can be instructive and motivational. If your parents did not, or are not, enjoying the quality of retirement that you feel they should, then learn from their mistakes. When I look out across the country I see too many examples of elderly people who worked hard their entire lives, who raised children to be good citizens, people who are patriotic, caring, and giving, yet who failed to save and are forced to live lives less comfortably than they deserve.

> *You must take personal responsibility. You cannot change the circumstances, the seasons, or the wind, but you can change yourself. That is something you have charge of.*
>
> —JIM ROHN,
> motivational speaker
> and entrepreneur

Some of the most optimistic people are the same ones who say to themselves, "I will start saving when I make more money, and that will be soon." Yet time slips by, good intentions linger for years, and then, before they know it, decades have passed and it may be too late to start.

The "what" and "when" we spoke about in Chapter 1, along with the "why" that we have covered in this part, provide a wonderful foundation for thought. Use that list of goals and objectives you made—call them "dreams," if you like—with the time frame you attached to each goal as your starting point. Now create a

JUST FOR FUN . . .

Someday I want to be rich. Some people get so rich they lose all respect for humanity. That's how rich I want to be.

—RITA RUDNER,
comedienne

picture-based dream book. Use images that elicit an emotional response, and show it to someone who will share your excitement and possibly help hold you accountable.

Continue to explore the question of why you are investing. Remind yourself frequently of the benefits you will have received from employing discipline and delayed gratification. Review your progress on a regular basis, but not on a daily basis. Keep your values and life perspectives in order and on the focus of your investment decisions.

Questions to Ask Yourself

1. Have I been responsible for my finances?
2. When I think of financial freedom for me and my family, what do I see? What does *my* financial freedom look like?
3. I achieve what I focus on. What have I been focusing on? Is it time to change my focus?
4. How skilled am I at finances? If my skill-set is lacking, will I commit to learning what I need to know?
5. Discipline is a necessary attribute for a successful financial life. Am I willing to commit to a disciplined financial plan?

Wisdom's To-Do List

1. Write a note to yourself: "I take responsibility for my life and finances." Keep the note in your wallet or purse. Read it from time to time until the thought occurs to you naturally.

2. For many people, money and finances take a backseat to other areas of life. To be financially successful requires focus. Determine to be determined about money matters.

3. Commit to a self-education program. This book is a good start, but don't stop here. Discover more through consistent study.

ANCIENT ADVICE

ECCLESIASTES 5:10—Whoever loves money never has enough; whoever loves wealth is never satisfied with his income.

PROVERBS 22:29—Do you see a man skilled in his work? He will serve before kings; he will not serve before obscure men.

PROVERBS 21:5—The plans of the diligent lead to profit as surely as haste leads to poverty.

III. THE GOOD DEAL

It was his own fault. He should have risen from bed earlier. His mother had nudged him, coaxed him, even threatened him, but Abidan had no urge to rise from his sleeping pallet. His younger brother and sister had been up an hour before, broken the night's fast with dried fish, bread, and dates, then began their chores. Their absence left the house quiet, perfect for a few moments more sleep.

Something tickled his foot. He gave a gentle kick. A second later, someone was dragging Abidan across the stone floor. His father said nothing as he clutched Abidan's foot. Complaints fell on deaf ears. Zerah did not let go until he had dragged his son out the front door and into the small courtyard that fronted the house. As with all the homes in his neighborhood, the courtyard was where the family prepared its meals and ate. The smell of smoke from innumerable cook fires hung in the air.

Zerah released Abidan's foot, but before he could rise his father seized a water pitcher and poured its contents on Abidan's face. He knew better than to complain. Within minutes he had changed his clothing and was in the workshop clearing away the debris from yesterday's construction and sharpening the cutting tools. He rushed through everything. He had to. Abidan was to meet with the king again.

He took no time for the morning meal, took no time to apologize for being slothful. Finally, his father said his first word of the morning: "Go."

Abidan was sweating as he ran along the city paths trying to arrive at the palace on time. He chastised himself for being so lazy.

The now familiar face of the servant wore a frown. "You are late, boy."

"I am. It is my fault alone. I apologize."

"Save the apology for your king."

As before, the servant lead him through the massive building and again to the throne room. Abidan froze at the door. Solomon sat in the judgment seat, and two men about the age of his father stood before the king. Abidan waited on the threshold as the servant introduced him.

Solomon turned his head; his eyes looked like cold river stones. He pointed at Abidan, then motioned for him to enter. Abidan wasted no more of the king's time.

"O King, may you live forever. I apologize for being late—"

"Hush, boy. Sit." He pointed at the lowest step of the raised platform. Abidan plopped down, grateful the king allowed him to stay. Questions filled his mind. Why were these two men here? Abidan knew the king sat as judge over disputes. The most pressing question was: Why was he, the poor son of a carpenter, allowed to be present?

"We may begin," Solomon said. "You, Kenan, bring the complaint. I will hear from you first."

"Yes, O King. I have been wronged, lied to, misled, and have lost what little fortune I had to this man." He pointed at the other man, a tall, lanky man with a smooth face. His accuser's face, however, bore the deep lines of those who spent their days in the beating sun. His beard bore more gray than the other man's, but Abidan judged him to be younger.

"That is untrue, O great King—"

A harsh glance from Solomon made the man go mute. The king returned his attention to Kenan. "Continue." He sounded bored.

"My king, just judge of all Israel, I believe this man should pay every bit of what I invested through him."

"You gave money to Aziel as an investment?"

"I did, O King. He promised me riches made in a short time, but he lied to me, took my money, and I have made no riches."

Abidan heard a soft groan rumble from Solomon.

"How do you answer, Aziel?"

"My king, wise and true, what Kenan says is a lie. I gave him an opportunity to make more than he has ever made in his miserable life, but he was too lazy to work my plan."

"And what is that plan, Aziel?"

"I am certain the king will see the great wisdom in this idea. As the king knows, pilgrims from the north country and many from the remote portions of the southern parts of the kingdom come to Jerusalem during the holy seasons, especially Passover and the Feast of the Tabernacles. Many come to celebrate and to make sacrifices at the Temple." Aziel smiled. "One day, while watching pilgrims at the temple, it occurred to me that many of them have need for sacrificial animals. As you know, O King, many types of animals are used in the sacrifices, and many of the pilgrims suffer loss on their journeys, forced to find new lambs or doves."

"And you sell such animals to the pilgrims?" Solomon asked.

"Not directly, O King. I have made arrangements to buy such animals at a discount, and others sell them for me. They buy the animals from me, then sell them to the travelers."

"And you make income through their sales?"

"Yes, O King."

Solomon turned to Kenan. "You may respond."

"He has not told the whole of it, King. He required that I buy more than I could sell. He also sold to my competition. I made some sales but not enough to earn back my initial investment. He tells me I am lazy, but I worked from sunup to sundown every day."

"If I may, my king. I am a generous man. My dear wife tells me I give too much away. I offered Kenan and all who work with me the opportunity to recruit people to work under them, and if they do, I allow them to share in the profit they make."

"I have heard enough," Solomon said. "Kenan."

"Yes, O King."

"You have been a fool. You entered into an agreement that could only lead to ruin. Why did you accept such an offer?"

The man looked as if someone had pierced him with a spear. "I was promised a quick profit for little work."

"And you believed that?" Solomon shook his head. "Did it not seem to you too good to be true?"

The man lowered his head.

Solomon continued. "He who works his land will have abundant food, but the one who chases fantasies will have his fill of poverty" [Proverbs 28:19]. He paused. "Do you understand the proverb, Kenan?"

"I think so, O King."

"Abidan, explain the proverb."

An arrow of fear struck Abidan's heart. He stood, amazed that he could achieve such a feat as standing. "Yes, my king." He faced Kenan and tried not to shake. A thirteen-year-old boy was considered a man, but it was improper for someone of such few years to lecture an elder. "The king's proverb means the wise man is one who works hard at his business and does not believe promises of wealth from strangers." Abidan faced the king to see if he had done a proper job. The king nodded.

"Another proverb, Kenan: He who walks with the wise grows wise, but a companion of fools suffers harm" [Proverbs 13:20]. When Solomon

spoke the word "fools," he turned his face to Aziel. "Does the boy need to explain the proverb?"

Both men said no.

Solomon straightened in his throne. "Kenan and Aziel, hear my decree. You, Kenan, have let greed guide you. Because of this I will not find in your favor. What you have lost you have lost. Perhaps you have now gained more in wisdom than you lost in money."

Kenan lowered his head. "Yes, King."

Abidan saw a broad smile cross Aziel's face. It evaporated the moment Solomon turned his attention to the man. "I do not want to see your face again, Aziel, especially in this room. Kenan's greed clouded his vision. Your greed has stripped away your honor. If you have any wisdom left, Aziel, you will think again of what you have done and the damage you have caused. Leave me—now."

Aziel opened his mouth as if to speak, then changed his mind. Abidan thought it a very wise decision. Aziel walked from the room without looking back.

"Kenan, you came to me for justice. You do not believe you have received it. Perhaps one day you will. You may go."

After Kenan exited, Solomon rose from the elevated throne and descended to the floor. "You have questions, Abidan?"

"I am not wise enough to understand what I have seen."

"You think my decision a poor one. You feel that I should have made Aziel return Kenan's money. Am I correct?"

"As always, my king."

"Who forced Kenan to enter into the agreement with Aziel?"

"No one, King. He decided to do so himself, but Aziel made false promises."

Solomon shook his head. "The promises were not false, but they were exaggerated, something Kenan should have seen. Did Aziel's scheme seem wise to you?"

"No, King."

"Good. Did we not learn that a man is responsible for his own actions and his own business?"

"Yes, King."

"I would have done no favor to Kenan by forcing Aziel to repay the money. Perhaps Kenan will be wiser even though poorer."

"But will Aziel not continue to do the same to others?"

"I suspect that is true, Abidan. There are many who look for the fast way to riches, the quick path to wealth. In the end it costs them more than they gain. Aziel will suffer for his actions. Men like him always do. Finish this sentence, Abidan: 'If there were an easy way to wealth and security, then . . .'"

Abidan thought for a moment. ". . . then everyone would be rich and secure."

"Yes, Abidan. The wise way is not the easy way to wealth, but it is the straightest way. Do you understand?"

"I do, O King."

"Then go help your father."

Abidan started to leave.

"One last thing, son. Do not make me wait again."

Abidan smiled. "I promise, my king."

CHAPTER 3

"PROMISES, PROMISES"

IN A NUTSHELL: Don't be naive.

If it sounds too good to be true, it probably is.

—ANONYMOUS

I f it sounds too good to be true . . ."

It usually happens late at night during those times when we can't sleep. After counting backward, counting sheep, counting marks on the ceiling, and thinking of all the things that need to be done tomorrow, we surrender to the fact that sleep isn't coming anytime soon. We get out of bed, head straight to the fridge for a little snack, and then turn on the television. With the glow of the screen the only light in the room, we scan the seemingly endless channels to find the one thing remotely interesting is an infomercial. There, in the middle of the night, we listen to someone promise us riches through his proven moneymaking plan. He touts. He hawks. He convinces us that we are just a phone call away from success. A few days later, UPS leaves a package at our front door.

We tell ourselves that we were caught in a weak moment. We also tell ourselves that it might be better if others didn't know we had bought the sales pitch.

I intentionally use the plural pronouns because many of us have bought into these scams at least once. The creators of these infomercials are a clever bunch. They know what we want: to be thin (without working hard); to look fabulous; to have beautiful skin; and, most of all, to be rich. So they give us a pitch and sell us a promise.

I want to focus on Solomon's lesson about getting rich. You might know where I'm going with this. Get-rich-quick proponents make it look so good . . . and so easy. Just follow some simple steps and you too can have it all: the fancy cars, the mansion, and the magnificent boat moored at your private dock. Who wouldn't want all of that?

Does anyone really make money doing this? Yep—the guy who is selling you his "magic" idea does. Anyone else? My guess is no. Sorry. You see, if it were easy, everyone would be rolling in cash.

King Solomon said, "He who works his land will have abundant food, but the one who chases fantasies will have his fill of poverty" (Proverbs 28:19).

Why is it we learn some lessons quickly while taking far too long to comprehend others? As a child you touched the hot stove once; it was enough—lesson learned. You burned your hand and that was it. Most of us have trouble believing the age-old saying "If it sounds too good to be true, it probably is." If we're not careful, we will be forced to relearn it again and again. Why do we believe those who sell such things? Are they seemingly so sincere that we have a hard time believing they would mislead us just to line their own pockets?

It is normal to want nice things. It is also understandable that we would follow those who, we have been told, have already achieved the things that we desire. The key here is to develop *discernment*.

DISCERNING DISCERNMENT

The Chinese are famous for saying that wisdom is attained through age. When my wife and I were traveling through Beijing we often saw younger people on bikes transporting an elderly person seated on a makeshift platform behind their seat. The reverence shown to older folks was inspiring and humbling, especially relative to how our society tends to discard the elderly.

How is it that these people achieve wisdom simply by living a long time? From my perspective, long life allows us to be taken advantage of enough times that we finally learn to discern between things that are too good to be true and those that deliver real return.

Listen to Solomon again. "A simple man believes anything, but a prudent man gives thought to his steps" (Proverbs 14:15).

When we turn to the "professional" investment industry, we must don the armor of prudence and discernment. I wrote a great deal about the commission-based investment brokerage industry in my previous book, *Demystifying Wall Street: Shedding a Little Light on the BULL!* I think there are a few things we can cover here that will cast light on investment mistakes.

Not unlike the infomercial creators, those at the top of investment brokerage firms are very smart people. They work with advertising experts to craft commercials and other forms of advertising depicting those two emotions that seem to encompass all others: fear and greed.

We fear making mistakes related to important goals such as our retirement. We fear working our entire lives only to be left with too little to live on. We fear that the overwhelming amount of investment information is simply too much for us to understand.

On the other side of the emotional coin, what we desire is relatively simple. The advertisers all know that retiring to a beachfront home or golfing community looks really good after a lifetime of work. Dancing the night away with our spouse after a fine meal and strolling hand in hand along the teak deck of a magnificent cruise ship has a certain appeal.

The brokerage firms, with the assistance of their advertising partners, lead us to believe that *with their help* we can achieve these things and avoid all obstacles in our way. Once they have created a connection between our hopes and dreams bound to the belief that they can help us, we become like sheep led to, well, pasture or slaughter.

Once the emotional bond is forged, these brilliant financiers pitch their products—investment opportunities—they are certain we will buy. Why wouldn't we? We trust them.

The creation of an investment product is strongly linked to the emotions of fear and greed that caused us to grace their finely polished doors in the first place. These are the same emotions that are cleverly interwoven throughout these investment ideas. Have you

> *Too many of us look upon Americans as dollar chasers. This is cruel libel, even it is reiterated thoughtlessly by the Americans themselves.*
>
> —ALBERT EINSTEIN, physicist

noticed how your broker calls with an investment idea that seems just perfect for the current market?

Notice how easy this is in the following example.

Frank D. is an investor, seeking growth of his portfolio for a much anticipated retirement just five years down the road. He is feeling the pressure of growing his nest egg as much as possible because once he retires Frank has no plans to reenter the workforce. He's been there, done that, and now it's time to start reaping the benefits of a lifetime of work.

The market has been good for the last few years. Frank's portfolio has grown nicely, but recently things have started getting bumpy. Frank reads in the newspaper about troubles in the housing market. The nightly TV news anchor is talking about higher unemployment numbers and a potential slowdown in the economy. He hears the radio talk-show host spouting off terms like GDP (gross domestic product), CPI (consumer price index), GNP (gross national product), ISM (factory orders manufacturing survey), and other numbers Frank doesn't understand.

Frank is uncertain what it all means, but he's sure it doesn't sound good for his retirement plans. He calls his broker to get some insight, which the man will surely provide even if he has no idea about Frank's situation. The broker promises to do a bit of research on Frank's behalf and get back to him tomorrow. This sounds good to Frank. Someone is working on the problem for him. He goes about his business knowing that an "expert" is looking into the matter just for him.

Frank's phone rings at nine a.m. the next day, and his broker says he has found "just the right investment to meet your needs." The broker offers an investment that will provide for "most" of the upside should the markets rise yet will protect Frank's money one hundred percent should the markets fall. The investment also just happens to have a five-year time horizon, which matches the time Frank expects to retire. What a coincidence.

With that brief description, he says, "Let's go ahead with it." The broker places the trade—then calculates the commission he just earned.

Did Frank do his homework? Did he take the time to understand the risks and fees associated with this "too good to be true" investment? Did he ask, "Are there any strings attached?"

Don't get me wrong. This investment might be a good one for Frank. The problem is, he didn't do his homework. He heard something that sounded good and jumped. Is that how King Solomon would have done it?

The investment industry is huge. We're talking trillions of dollars. It is crammed with highly skilled *salespeople*, usually called advisers. The vast majority of these advisers are paid on commissions. These commission dollars are generated by selling investment products to consumers like you. These "consumers" are the investors.

When choosing investments, you must do your homework. Choose wisely when selecting an adviser and even then, just because an investment is recommended, it doesn't mean it's the best choice for you. The one thing to remember when evaluating such offers is that there is no perfect investment, no matter how enticing the product is made to seem. Truth is, investing is hard work.

Remember, if it were easy, then everyone would do it.

I want to encourage you to "sleep on it." Until you have developed the ability to recognize what may be false promises, until you can reliably sniff out inauthentic sales practices, take time before making a decision. It's amazing how different a situation or purchase may seem after a night or two of good sleep.

Solomon has more advice for us: "He that hastens to be rich has an evil eye, and considers not that poverty shall come upon him" (Proverbs 28:22).

Can you imagine how much money has been lost by those of us who responded to a pressure-filled sales scam? The number is probably in the billions. They told us that this opportunity must be decided upon NOW. "This opportunity of a lifetime will be gone tomorrow."

When we consider these things with a rational, relaxed state of mind, we can avoid such nonsense. Still it happens. It may well have happened to you. You may feel ashamed that you have fallen for such a ploy. Please don't consider my words condescending. I am a fellow traveler. I too have bought into a scam that seemed so right, so intelligent, such a good deal, that I fell for it with absolute confidence. So I don't preach—I share what I've learned with you.

There was a time in my life when I was determined to better my body and my athletic ability. I dedicated two hours per day to running, swimming, cycling, and a great deal of weightlifting.

> JUST FOR FUN . . .
>
> *With money in your pocket, you are wise and you are handsome and you can sing well too.*
>
> —YIDDISH PROVERB

I scrutinized everything that went into my mouth. I became a perfect target for an MLM (multilevel marketing) company in—what else?—supplements and foods designed for better health, increased and sustained energy, and maximum nutrition.

I was sold on the integrity of this company, on the research behind the products, and on the fact that simply by personally using these products and sharing the results with others, customers would flock to my door to order their supplies, making me rich.

Repeat after me: "If it sounds too good to be true, it probably is." And, "If it were this easy, everyone would do it."

Do I need to tell you the outcome? The whole thing turned out to be a sales scam. Sure, the products tasted good, but that was it. The "sincere" person who recruited me into the whole thing was a former assistant district attorney who, as it turns out, seemed to lie every time his lips moved. My income had a lot of zeros in it—nothing in front of the zeros, but lots of zeros. I was more than embarrassed; I was mortified. When I left the MLM, my sponsor tried to extort money from me, tried to have me fired from my real job, and harassed my family at all hours of the night. Yes, this was a former assistant district attorney. We had to file a restraining order to keep him away. This finally worked when our attorneys threatened continuing lawsuits. I went through all this simply because of my greed and desire for a shortcut to wealth.

Yes, greed is a powerful motivator for stupid decisions. Although it falls into a slightly different category, there is another factor to consider: financial hardship.

STRESS IS A LOUSY FINANCIAL PARTNER

For the person in a difficult and stressful financial position, the enticing sales pitch is appealing not only because it promises the participant a way to get rich, but also because it appears to be a way for him to get his head above water. This person wants to pay off pressing bills and stop the collectors from calling. It's not about big houses, shiny new boats, or bright red sports cars for him—it's about survival.

The late singer/songwriter Dan Fogelberg described what it feels like to be in this situation. In the song "Loose Ends," he wrote:

Climbing a mountain in darkness,
Stranded alone on the ledge,
Every attempt that I make to hang on pushes me nearer
the edge.
Sensing the changes impending,
My thoughts are diffused by despair,
I feel like I'm swimming straight up under water,
Desperately racing for air.

Like me, you may find those words meaningful. I understand; I have been there.

Fogelberg goes on to talk about those times when he had plenty, and may have been accumulating too much. In the same song he wrote:

Surrounding myself with possessions,
I surely have more than I need.
I don't know if this is justice hard earned,
or simply a matter of greed.

Fogelberg got it. On both sides. It took a while and a few mistakes, but I finally got it too.

When we find ourselves in a difficult financial situation, we are more susceptible to investment and/or business promises.

Let's examine a common "business opportunity" that many who are searching for an answer, any answer, tend to fall into. This is the world of multilevel marketing (MLM). MLM makes claims of financial growth, free time, fantastic incomes, travel, and all the fine points life has to offer. Does this sound like something you would like? I would. Any chance this sounds too good to be true?

In 1979, the Federal Trade Commission (FTC) issued a decision, *In re Amway Corporation*, that indicated that multilevel marketing was not illegal per se. The commission did, however, find Amway guilty of price fixing (by requiring "independent" distributors to sell at the low price) and *making exaggerated income claims.*

Another criticism is that MLM programs are set up to make most distributors fail, as there is an incentive to continue to recruit distributors even as the products have reached market saturation, thus causing the average earnings per distributor to fall.[1]

Solomon's take on this? "A prudent man sees danger and takes refuge, but the simple keep going [after it]" (Proverbs 22:3).

I believe that the "simple" keep going after it because they want to believe there is a way out of their financial mess. Once again, most of us want to believe that those who promise to help us improve our situation are sincere. The reality is most of these programs are not in your best interest.

PROMISES, PROMISES

In his piece titled *"Ten Big Lies of Multilevel Marketing,"* Robert Fitzpatrick states:

Unfortunately, the MLM business model is a hoax that is hidden beneath misleading slogans. Calling it a "great business opportunity" makes no more sense than calling the purchase

---

1. Dean Van Druff, "What's Wrong with Multi-Level Marketing?" http://www.vandruff.com/mlm.html.

of a lottery ticket a "business venture" and winning the lottery a "viable income opportunity for everyone." MLM industry claims of distributor income potential, its glorified descriptions of the "network" business model, and its prophecies of dominating product distribution have as much validity in business as UFO sightings do in the realm of science.[2]

As in all pyramid schemes, the incomes of those distributors at the top and the profits to the sponsoring corporations come from a continuous influx of new investors at the bottom. Viewed superficially in terms of company profits and the wealth of an elite group at the pinnacle of the MLM industry, the model can appear viable to the uninformed, just as all pyramid schemes do before they collapse or are prosecuted by authorities.

The growth of MLM is the result of deceptive marketing that plays upon treasured cultural beliefs, social and personal needs, and some economic trends, rather than its ability to meet any consumer needs. The deceptive marketing is nurtured by a general lack of professional evaluation or investigation by reputable business media. Consequently, there is widespread belief that MLM is a viable business investment or career choice for nearly everyone and that the odds of financial success in the venture are comparable or better than other employment or business ventures.

MLM's true constituency is not the consuming public but hopeful investors. The market for these investors grows significantly in times of economic transition, globalization, and employee displacement. Promises of quick and easy financial

---

2. Robert L. Fitzpatrick, "Ten Big Lies of Multilevel Marketing." www.mlmwatch.org.

deliverance and the linking of wealth to ultimate happiness also play well in this market setting. The marketing thrust of MLM is directed to prospective distributors, rather than product promotions to purchasers. Its true products are not long-distance phone services, vitamins, or skin creams, but the investment propositions for distributorships which are deceptively portrayed with images of high income, low time requirements, small capital investments, and early success.

I place fault on no one for falling victim to these programs. The lure is powerful. Our earnest desire to better our financial position and to provide nice things for our loved ones makes us a target for any number of schemes.

For me, the worst outcome of failed attempts to better one's situation is the high toll it takes on the emotions. It is common for the participant to be told the failure is their fault. They're accused of not trying hard enough. Participants are often embarrassed at sales meetings.

The reality is that, again quoting Fitzpatrick, "For almost everyone who invests, MLM turns out to be a losing financial proposition. Fewer than 1 percent of all MLM distributors ever earn a profit, and those earning a sustainable living at this business are a much smaller percentage still."

So don't feel bad. You're not alone.

JUST FOR FUN . . .

A wise man should have money in his head, but not in his heart.

—JONATHAN SWIFT,
author

You see, when it comes to making money, either through investing our savings or seeking business opportunities, we have a lot to learn, and the wise teachings of King Solomon can help.

There is no sin in trying to

better our financial life. The failing comes from allowing greed to cloud our judgment. Let us be wise, just as Solomon is teaching Abidan.

The hallmarks of a good investment tend to be somewhat boring and predictable but tried and true. The investment industry continually brings forth fancy (they say sophisticated) newfangled investment ideas because we tend to think of new as better.

WE AIN'T DONE IT THIS WAY BEFORE— AND FOR GOOD REASON

Consider all the "new" limited partnerships brought to market in the 1980s. Wow, did they sound good. How many of them are still around today? The answer is next to none. The only things lingering from these investments are the lawsuits.

Then in the 1990s, the industry convinced us that with the advent of technology the world had changed. Industries that made money for a hundred years were now passé. The smart money was focused almost entirely on technology stocks.

In their haste to sell us—and sell us they did—the latest industry products that would certainly make us all rich, they must have conveniently forgotten a few simple rules of mathematics and investing. Things like that when prices get too high, they *always* tend to come down. We call this "reversion to the mean."

I remember attending a dinner meeting where I heard from industry executives that "this time it's different," and that—now get this—"the old metrics [mathematics] have changed." They said that the old ways of investing, the way of folks like Warren Buffett, were now like dinosaurs and would be replaced forever by the "new" economy.

Can you believe the arrogance? The last I checked, tech stocks crashed huge starting in March 2000, and Warren Buffett, the old dinosaur, is now one of the two richest men in the world. So much for the brilliant Wall Street gurus. But here's the rub: They made a fortune selling this garbage.

Finally, as I write this in 2008, we are suffering from a complete meltdown of the mortgage and housing markets. Wall Street did it again. They packaged and repackaged junk mortgages, mortgages that they knew had no way of being repaid, into fancy new investment products. They restructured the junk so far from its original form that investors had no idea what they were buying. The industry went so far as to have much of this nonsense receive a rating of AAA.

I can assure you we will be hearing of lawsuits from this fiasco for years to come. As I write this, the firm Bear Stearns is no longer, as it was purchased, with the help of the Federal Reserve, by Morgan Stanley. Lehman Brothers recently filed for bankruptcy, and Merrill Lynch is in the process of being sold to Bank of America.

Yet if we will take time to learn from these mistakes, we can find gems of current wisdom. For instance, during all this, how did the long-established (dinosaurs) invest their money? Without going into great detail, which you can learn for yourself by reading their books, they bought into companies that had been around for decades, companies in which the investor understood what the company was selling and how they were making a profit.

These skilled investors avoided "new" investment products. At the very least, they looked upon these latest and greatest investment ideas with a good deal of skepticism.

Maybe you feel too overwhelmed and unskilled in this area to be able to discern for yourself the difference between a sound investment or business idea and a bad one. Fear not. In the next chapter, we will again learn wisdom from Solomon concerning the wise use of advisers. Even in the case of seeking council, we must have discernment. Thank goodness we have a wonderful teacher available to help show us the way.

Questions to Ask Yourself

1. Is the investment I am about to make one that my mentors, those whom I respect, would likely make?
2. Does this investment or business opportunity seem just a bit too good to be true?
3. Am I being told that this program is easy?
4. Is there a long history for this investment or business idea?
5. Does this feel like some new/creative way to try to beat the market?

Wisdom's To-Do List

1. Take time with your decisions. Ask questions of yourself and of others "in the know."
2. Skepticism can be a powerful ally. Don't be afraid to be a financial skeptic.
3. While new opportunities are exciting, tried-and-true methods are more secure. Before investing in something with no track record, decide if you can afford to lose the money.

ANCIENT ADVICE

PROVERBS 28:19—He who works his land will have abundant food, but the one who chases fantasies will have his fill of poverty.

PROVERBS 14:15—A simple man believes anything, but a prudent man gives thought to his steps.

PROVERBS 22:3—A prudent man sees danger and takes refuge, but the simple keep going and suffer for it.

PROVERBS 1:19—Such is the end of all who go after ill-gotten gain [greed]; it takes away the lives of those who get it.

IV. THE KING'S ADVISERS

Abidan arrived early. This time he was shown to the portico. Although he had now made several visits to the palace compound, he still felt lost in its size and complexity. The palace, as everyone in Jerusalem knew, consisted of more than one building. Four primary structures made up the bulk of the king's palace. Abidan had yet to see the many rooms and service areas.

"To the throne room today?" Abidan asked the servant who met him at each arrival.

"No." The servant offered nothing more, and Abidan didn't think it wise to press the man.

Servants moved with quiet intensity. Men dressed in expensive robes walked by. Abidan did his best to avoid eye contact. A carpenter's son had no right to gaze upon men of such importance.

Abidan followed three paces behind the servant until the man led him to an exterior wall. Window openings covered with cedar lattice lined the partition. The servant pushed open two tall, thick wood doors, and Abidan found himself outside again. What lay before him stole his breath.

When he first met Solomon, the king had been in a small courtyard with stone benches and a fountain. Abidan believed the courtyard to be one of the most beautiful things he had ever seen—until now.

"The king is in the portico. Do not approach him unless he calls for you. Do you understand?"

"Yes, I understand."

The servant motioned for Abidan to cross the threshold. The moment he did, the servant closed the doors. Abidan stood alone, surrounded by tall stone columns with thick cedar beams spanning the distance between them. To one side was a shallow, wide, and long reflecting pool. Several birds drank from the pool's edge. A peacock strolled by as if he owned everything in sight. A tall wall marked off the perimeter, constructed of three rows of large, hand-hewed stones and topped with thick cedar beams.

Abidan moved through the open space slowly. He could smell the sweetness of the air, perfumed by flowering plants. Abidan felt as if he had entered the Garden of Eden.

Between the rows of columns, wide flat white stones had been laid, forming a level surface for walking.

Abidan raised his eyes and gazed down the long portico. At the end was a covered structure, and at its center sat a large chair, thronelike, but more simple in design. Solomon sat on the throne. Surrounding him were three men: two younger than Abidan's father and one who appeared older.

He took several steps closer. Abidan could hear their voices but could not make out their words. The older man was animated, pointing at the two younger men. Solomon leaned forward on his chair, listening intently to what was being said.

Abidan stopped, not wanting to approach without being summoned. The servant's warning rang in his ears. Still, he felt conflicted. He was due to meet with Solomon and didn't want to be late, nor did he wish to interrupt the king. He settled on standing within sight of the king but making no motion to draw Solomon's attention away from whatever business was before him. He chose patience.

Solomon's head swiveled from side to side, as he listened to the men before him. The two younger men stood to Solomon's right; the elderly man, to the king's left. Finally the king looked up and made eye contact with Abidan. He rose, said something to the three men, motioned to the side, and stepped from the covered area into the open arcade. He hadn't taken three steps before servants appeared with platters of food and goblets of drink. The three men helped themselves.

"Have I kept you waiting, Abidan?"

"Only moments, my king. I could see you were busy."

Solomon chuckled. It was the first time Abidan had seen him do so. "Yes, there is much that demands my attention."

"The men with you seem upset. Are you judging their dispute?" He paused, then quickly added, "If it is permissible for me to ask."

"You are observant, Abidan, and that skill will serve you well."

"Thank you, O King."

"You are also wrong."

"Wrong?"

Solomon put a hand on the boy's shoulder and guided him along the stone path between the pillars. "They have a dispute, but not like you saw the other day. They work for me."

"I see."

"Not yet, but you will." Solomon stepped to the reflecting pool and sat on its edge. Abidan joined him. "What did you notice about the three men?"

"One looks old, two are younger."

"Looks old?" Solomon gazed up the path and stared at the men. "Yes, he looks old for a reason—he is old."

"I meant no disrespect," Abidan said.

"He is proud of his age, as he should be. His name is Jada and he

is one of my chief builders. You have heard of the aqueduct I am building?"

"Yes, O King. It is well known throughout the land."

"Jada is in charge of its construction. The other two men are his assistants."

"Yet they argue with him?"

"They are passionate about the work they do. The aqueduct will be there long after all of us have gone the way of our fathers."

Abidan stared at the ground. The thought of a time after King Solomon's death saddened him.

"Enosh and Shobi have a new idea about how to span a small valley. They wish to alter the path of the aqueduct. Jada believes it is a bad decision. I have agreed with Enosh and Shobi, but Jada tells me I am wrong."

The revelation surprised Abidan. "This man tells you that you are mistaken? You are the wisest man who has ever lived."

"Do you think a wise man is always correct, Abidan?"

Abidan recognized the tone. The lesson had begun. After a moment's thought he realized the lesson began the moment he arrived. "I have always thought so, O King."

"A wise man is a man who listens to wisdom other than his own. Jada has given me good counsel over the years."

"But King, you said that you agreed with the other two men."

"I did say that, Abidan, but I have learned some things. What I tell you now, I say in confidence. You must not repeat the words. Can I trust you?"

"Yes."

"To alter the planned course of the aqueduct means crossing the property of several people. We would have to buy that land. Enosh and Shobi have family who would benefit from the sale of their property. No doubt, some of that profit would go to Enosh and Shobi."

"So they earn riches."

"Correct."

Abidan thought for a moment. "They have advised you to do something that benefits only them?"

"Not only. There is some wisdom in their suggestion, but their motivation has nothing to do with building a successful aqueduct. Before I learned of their plan, I believed they offered wise counsel. Then Jada came to me. What do you learn from this?"

"Never lie to the king."

Again, Solomon chuckled. "Very true, but your answer is lacking. Learn this proverb: Plans fail for lack of counsel, but with many advisers they succeed" [Proverbs 15:22].

Abidan let the words roll in his mind. "The wise man knows that wisdom is found in the advice of others."

"You are getting good at this, Abidan. You are correct, but there is more. Remember, Enosh and Shobi advised me, and their advice seemed at first very sound."

"But you learned they had something to gain in the advice they gave."

"Exactly. Jada gave good advice and his motivation was the success of our project and nothing more. I pay him well for his work. He has no need to trick me."

"Advice, then, O King, is best when it comes from someone who is wise and not greedy."

"True. The wise man learns whom he can trust and only then listens to advice." Solomon rose. "I must return."

"My king, may I ask what will become of Enosh and Shobi?"

Abidan felt as if Solomon's stare could see straight through him.

"No."

CHAPTER 4

"ASK THE WISE"

He that won't be counseled can't be helped.

— BENJAMIN FRANKLIN,

American statesman

D on't go it alone.

God bless Americans. We are a caring, compassionate, and engaging people. We stand for the right. We fight for the oppressed. We respond to needs, anywhere in the world. We give of our money and our time, and even our blood. We let our voices be heard against injustice. And one other thing: We have opinions about everything.

When it comes to sports, we freely tell the coach how to manage the game and run his team. We let the players know when we feel they aren't working hard enough. When the wrong play is called, we let them know that, too. How could they be so stupid? Why is it that we in the stands or watching on TV can so clearly see the right play and they can't?

Likewise, taxi drivers freely share their opinions with us on topics such as how our government is run, who the next president should be, how to better manage the war, how to end world hunger, and why the judges picked the wrong woman for Miss America.

If you want an opinion about most anything there is someone dying to give you theirs.

LISTEN, BUT LISTEN TO THE RIGHT PEOPLE

Once, while sitting in some airport, en route to somewhere, I had a few free moments before catching my next flight—just enough time to have my shoes shined. I hoped I could sit in silence and enjoy an example of the age-old art of shoe-shining. The gentleman shiner asked about my profession. When I told him I was an investment manager, his face showed an eagerness to *share* his thoughts with me on international investing. I've received advice from people in every walk of life. It's always interesting but not always helpful. I bet you've had the same experience.

Solomon states, "All a man's ways seem right to him" (Proverbs 21:2). That's for sure. Everyone is entitled to his or her opinion, yet just because a belief is held doesn't make it truth. Likewise, simply because one believes a position is false doesn't make truth any less true.

The question at hand is: How can we discern wisdom from mere opinion? Is there a difference? Should we consider a person who has shown considerable wisdom in one area of life an "expert" in every other area of life?

When it comes to managing our investments, this becomes an important challenge. Many sources of investment opinion are truly "invested" in offering a specific opinion. You ask, "How so?" Good question, and one I hope to answer in this section.

A few years back, I was having dinner in upstate New York with Andy Rooney of the CBS television show *60 Minutes*. It was a magnificent fall evening. The leaves were changing, and a brisk yet not uncomfortable breeze reminded us that winter was near. Our table was in the backyard of a prominent real estate developer's home.

Mr. Rooney and I were both friends of this gentleman. Actually, I was simply a business associate and Andy was his next-door neighbor, but on that particular evening we felt like friends.

As we dined by candlelight and moonlight, Andy and I found we had a number of things in common, including an appreciation of good red wine. I did much of the initial talking, mostly in response to Andy's questions about the country's financial situation and how an investor could profit from it. As we talked, Andy continued to enjoy the fruit of the vine.

When it was Andy's turn to carry the conversation he was primed for action. Along with the few other guests, I found myself on the receiving end of a number of *60 Minutes*-style tirades. It was as if I were living inside a greatest-hits record. Mr. Rooney, or Andy—we were clearly on a first-name basis after our second bottle of wine—was on a roll. His rants made their way to the investment industry.

Andy asked—and then answered—in the way only Andy Rooney could, "What do stockbrokers do? They don't seem to *make* anything, or for that matter they don't seem to *build* anything, either. They merely offer opinions. The way I see it, they are paid obscene amounts of money whether they are right or wrong."

With that statement still hanging in the air, he took another sip of wine. Others laughed, yet I immediately knew he was right. I responded, "To add insult to injury, stockbrokers are paid more and more commissions in order to offer more and more opinions."

Andy looked at me as if to say, "You get it, don't you?" I nodded. His rant was not intended to be a joke, but an insight.

It is important that investors look deeply into the motivation of the advice giver and ask the following: Who is the primary beneficiary of this advice? Is the advice given solely for the benefit of the receiver, or is there a behind-the-scenes motivation?

For example, think for a moment about your doctor. Can you imagine if he or she dispensed medical advice based on the commission the advice paid? What if each time your doctor recommended a procedure, you had to wonder if the procedure was for *his* benefit or *yours*? We're talking colonoscopies.

This is the same thing we are discussing here, merely substituting your financial health for your medical health.

Are you receiving good advice? Is your adviser looking out for your best interest, or his? Is it wise to blindly follow advice without first discerning the quality and motivation behind the opinion?

Solomon told us, "He who walks with the wise grows wise, but a companion of fools suffers harm" (Proverbs 13:20). So the question at hand seems to be: Do you walk with the wise or with fools?

Consider this: Newspapers are in the business of selling advertising. Television shows are in the same line of work. Financial newsletters sell subscriptions. The motivation of all three is the same: to make money. This, in and of itself, is not bad, and these sources of information can be helpful, yet you must always consider the source *and the motivation*.

Newsletters may be written by those who freely offer advice but have never held the responsibility of managing someone else's money. Making a recommendation is one thing, but making a recommendation and having to answer for it is quite another. The person who gives advice yet doesn't manage money has nothing to sell but a subscription to his newsletter.

On the other hand, a person who sells a newsletter and also provides money management services may be using the newsletter as a means of soliciting new clients to his money management business. Whom should you trust?

The answer lies in motivation more than the information. Newspapers, television, and newsletters can provide useful information and knowledge, but it is up to you to separate valid information from subtle sales strategy.

Dealing with a financial adviser is different. The trustworthy factor is more easily discerned. One question needs to be answered in order to evaluate the advice: Does the adviser earn a *commission* for your implementation of his advice? If the answer is yes, then how can you know who the real beneficiary of the advice is?

Feeling a bit discouraged? Don't. At least not yet, because it gets worse before it gets better—but it does get better. Let's continue with the bad news first, then we will look at some answers.

I have heard it said many times, "If I can't trust others with financial advice, then I will do it myself because I can certainly trust myself." So here's the bad news: We have a lot to learn about trusting ourselves.

FANCY TERMS AND SIMPLE IDEAS

Here are two very important lessons; the first is from me, the second from King Solomon. If you choose to believe only one, then please take the latter. (I don't suggest that my advice is on par with Solomon's.)

First, "If it were easy, everyone would be doing it." Second, as

Solomon said, "He who trusts in himself is a fool, but he who walks in wisdom is kept safe" (Proverbs 28:26). So what do we do now? Let's learn about ourselves.

There is a fascinating area of study called "behavioral finance." Numerous books and articles have been written on the subject. My intention here is simply to introduce you to the idea. Hopefully, this will spark your interest and help you to avoid the more common mistakes associated with "do it yourself" investing.

So what is behavioral finance? Albert Phung described it this way:

> According to conventional financial theory, the world and its participants are, for the most part, rational "wealth maximizers." However, there are many instances where emotion and psychology influence our decisions, causing us to behave in unpredictable or irrational ways. Behavioral finance is a relatively new field that seeks to combine behavioral and cognitive psychological theory with conventional economics and finance to provide explanations for why people make irrational financial decisions.[1]

Now doesn't that help to build your self-confidence in managing your own financial future? Let's take a look at just a few of the areas of behavioral finance you may find useful. Remember, there is a great deal being written on this subject that I think can help whether you invest by yourself or with the help of an adviser, so please feel free to dig in.

"Asymmetrical emotional response should equal asymmetrical

---

1. Albert Phung, Behavioral Finance: Introduction, Investopedia. http://www.investopedia.com/university/behavioral_finance/default.asp.

investment portfolio design." (I feel smart just writing that statement.) It is much simpler than it seems, so hang in here with me.

The emotion you experience when earning a 10 percent return on your investments is much different than the emotional response you have when losing 10 percent. Financially, the two amounts are the same yet we respond to them differently.

Try to remember a time when you learned your investments were up 10 percent. You probably cracked a smile, thought you were a genius, and walked away feeling pretty good. On the other hand, when most people become aware of a 10 percent decline in their investment value the response is more along the lines of "What did I do wrong?" Or, "This is going to be difficult to make up." Or, "I am going to fire my broker." Or, "My wife is going to kill me." Use whatever example you like, but the reality is that the emotion associated with gain is much different than the emotion associated with loss. This is what I mean by "asymmetrical." The two emotions are not equal.

To further examine this idea, you can apply this theory to almost any area of life that involves positive and negative results. Say your boss comes to you to talk about your salary. One possibility is that she offers you a 10 percent raise. Your response would probably be, "Cool, I could use the extra money." On the other hand, what if your employer said she needed to reduce your income by 10 percent? What do you think your response would be then? Would you be terribly disappointed? Would you be shocked? Would you start looking for another job?

Have I made the point? Emotions are not equal. Then how should you apply this idea to the design of your investments? How does this apply to investment advice?

First and foremost, you must understand your personal objectives and goals. Everyone I meet says, "I want maximum returns with little risk." I hate to break the news to you, but these are somewhat opposing goals. The key is to prioritize. It's not that you can't hope to achieve both of these targets, but one must take priority over the other.

Let me share a huge secret. Your priority should be to protect your money. In order for compounding to be effective you must protect against loss. Think of it this way: If you start with one hundred dollars to invest and lose 50 percent, you now have fifty dollars. Pretty simple math so far. Here is where it gets tricky. What percentage gain do you need to recover that 50 percent loss? Not 50 percent, but 100 percent of what remains. You need to double your money to make up the half that you lost.

Think about that the next time "free" advice is offered to you. The hard truth is making money is twice as hard as losing it. How do I go about investing money, or designing portfolios in order to match asymmetrical goals and emotions with actual investments? I use a number of alternative investments; for instance, hedge funds and long/short funds. I would suggest you learn a good deal about these types of investments before employing them in your portfolio.

Here is another theory to consider before making investment decisions on your own. It is called "investing with inertia." The idea is simple to understand. You may laugh at this one, but don't underestimate its power.

> *No man is so foolish but he may sometimes give another good counsel, and no man so wise that he may not easily err if he takes no other counsel than his own. He that is taught only by himself has a fool for a master.*
>
> —BEN JONSON,
> English dramatist and poet

Inertia investing is the belief that when the market is going up it will always go up, and when the market is going down it will always go down. Here are a few facts and stories to help you understand.

Think back to 1999. The stock markets were going up like crazy. Every time you turned on the TV a story would air about another twenty-something-year-old kid making millions of dollars, maybe hundreds of millions, when his Internet company went public. In addition, there were ads in newspapers, magazines, and newsletters touting mutual funds that were providing high double-digit returns to their investors. No one wanted to miss out on the riches to be had. In fact, even experienced financial "experts" were saying that the "rules of the game" had changed. It no longer mattered, so they said, if a company is profitable for it to make huge money; it just had to have a niche in the Internet age.

"The markets are going up fast so get on the train and hold on for the ride of your life." The financial press told us that if we couldn't make money in that market we were crazy. "This time it's different."

Do you see the emotional power that inertia thinking has on your investment decision-making process? How about this fact: During this madness more money flowed into technology-based mutual funds than at any time in history. Mutual fund flows help us identify those worrisome moments when investors fall head over heels for a particular sector. Just look at the tech bubble. In the five months from November 1999 to March 2000, $47 billion went into technology funds. By the end of March, tech-fund assets hit $163 billion. So one-third of the assets in these funds had been invested for six months or less. That indicates how the crowd can be really wrong at major inflection points.[2]

Do I need to remind you what happened over the next thirty

---

2. *BusinessWeek*, Mutual Fund Report, June 25, 2007.

months? The NASDAQ, which is the index that tracks primarily tech stocks, began a decline of approximately 75 percent.[3] As I write this in mid-2008, it still has not recovered to the value it was in March 2000. People thought the market was going up with no end in sight. The March 2000 cover of *Money* magazine said, "Invest in the Hottest Market EVER." This was about a week before one of the worst bear markets in history began.

Are you a believer yet?

Here is another example of inertia investing that covers the other side of the coin. It is not only when the market is rising that investors make bad decisions and advisers give faulty advice.

In October 2002, the market hit its low point for the cycle. The Dow had fallen some 32 percent, the S&P 500 had fallen some 45 percent,[4] and the U.S. stock markets were starting a new upward trend. This was one of the best times in years to buy back into the stock markets. Yet what did the average investor and adviser do? They bought bonds because they believed stocks would continue to fall (classic inertia investing). They had lost so much money they were not about to get burned again. Investors, on the advice of their advisers, poured more money into bond funds than at any other time in history.

This cycle of buying when stocks are going up and selling when stocks (or any type of investment) are going down is the opposite of what the great investors do. What skilled investors do is called *contrarian investing*. These wizards buy when everyone else is selling and sell when everyone else is buying. Seems logical, but this is very hard to do properly.

These two theories contained within the topic of behavioral

3. Calculated with Yahoo Finance Charting. www.yahoo.com/finance.
4. Calculated with Yahoo Finance Charting. www.yahoo.com/finance.

finance will hopefully help you filter out some of the investment advice noise. There are many more principles of behavioral finance, including hindsight bias (similar to inertia investing), herd behavior, overconfidence, and overreaction. As I said before, this area of study is of critical importance for the investor and adviser alike. I hope you will take the time to learn more about behavioral finance and how it affects you.

> *Seek ye counsel of the aged for their eyes have looked on the faces of the years and their ears have hardened to the voices of Life. Even if their counsel is displeasing to you, pay heed to them.*
>
> —KAHLIL GIBRAN, philosopher and poet

I suspect you are asking yourself the following questions: (1) How do I find reliable investment counsel? (2) If I can't trust my own decision-making abilities, then where do I go?

Before we get to some answers, here is one more type of advice you should be leery of. This type of advice isn't specific to investments per se, but is more predictive in nature. For instance, an economist may offer an opinion on how the economy should perform over the coming months or years. Another may offer an estimation of job creation or loss, housing starts, consumer spending or demand, the upcoming Christmas season sales numbers—you get the picture. This type of counsel may not specifically recommend an investment, but could certainly affect how your investments perform, or even may steer you toward other types of investments.

When I hear big-picture advice like that, which comes from economists, I think of something I heard a well-known financial expert say: "When I was growing up I always wanted to be an economist. Never wrong, simply revised." There is nothing wrong in listening to well-educated economists and financial experts, but their opinions—like *all* opinions—should be weighed carefully. Economists can revise a forecast; individual investors cannot revise past investments—they can only reevaluate and reinvest.

Statistics such as these are often revised numerous times over the course of years. As an investor, you should never make investment decisions based solely on this type of advice, but rather use these stats as one of many sources of information. This type of information should be used more to support your investment decision or potentially help to time the purchase or sale of an investment transaction.

WHOM SHOULD YOU CALL?

So where do you go for advice?

I have not tried to steer you away from these multiple sources of information, but to make you aware of your need to understand the motivation of advisers; to separate, as best you can, the useful advice from the advice given to earn a commission.

Once you learn—and it does take practice—to have your internal antenna tuned to the "They're selling me something here" channel, you will become skilled at separating useful advice from the "I want to influence you so I can make a commission" variety.

In the world of investment advice, I feel strongly that any person who may generate a commission connected with the advice given should be viewed with skepticism. The best foundation for an adviser-investor relationship is a flat-fee arrangement.

Let me take a moment to contrast flat-fee investment advice with its commission-based counterpart.

Let's say you have an IRA worth $200,000. You may have

worked for twenty to thirty years in order to accumulate this money. Is the money important to you? You bet it is. This may be all, or a significant part, of the money that must last you for *the rest of your days*. If you were to lose this money, how badly would it affect your life? We are talking about your future and possibly the future of your spouse, in addition to any gift you may want to leave to your children. Most likely this is the single most important "pool" of money you have ever had to manage.

When you seek out investment advice, you will have to pay for that advice. No problem so far. Generally, there are two ways you can go about paying that fee. The first, and by far most common, way is to engage a commission-based broker. This person may work for a large Wall Street investment firm or a small company, or even be an independent. The broker may even tell you that he can work either for a commission or on a fee-*based* program. Either way he receives a commission, and therefore you can never really be certain if the advice is given for your best interest or his.

If you choose to work with a fee-*only* adviser, and I am talking about an adviser who cannot legally accept a commission, then you and the adviser agree to an annual fee. This fee will most likely be a percentage of the total amount of your account.

For instance, using the $200,000 example above, should the two of you agree to a 1 percent annual fee for the investment advice, then your account will be charged $500 quarterly, adding up to $2,000 annually. Once the agreement has been made, then and for as long as the adviser is engaged to manage your account, you can be certain that all investments recommended and made on your behalf are implemented because the adviser believes they are in *your* best interest. The adviser has absolutely no conflicting incentive to do otherwise.

Now, if you are thinking that $2,000 seems like a lot of money, compare that to a typical mutual fund purchase into a fund that has a front-end fee of 5 percent. If the investment amount is $40,000, then you have already paid $2,000 in fees.

As an aside, even if the broker places you in a class B or C share mutual fund, which a fee-only adviser would never do, and tells you there is no front-end fee, the broker is still making more money, and that money is coming out of your account. You may not see it, but the fee is there.

So my answer to the dilemma of where to seek advice is this: Work through a fee-only adviser. Now, just because someone is a fee-only adviser doesn't necessarily make them an investment expert. You should still find someone with a long track record and who has clients you can ask for a referral. Generally speaking, I have found that fee-only advisers tend to be long-term industry professionals who have established a credible track record of success or they wouldn't choose this way of being compensated.

The fee-only platform tends to shift a good deal of the risk that you as the investor assume, and places the risk on the adviser. The adviser has no means of making a living from his practice unless he delivers a positive return in both customer service and investment performance.

Finally on this topic, our great teacher King Solomon said, "He who ignores discipline [instruction] comes to poverty and shame, but whoever heeds correction [counsel] is honored" (Proverbs 13:18). There is good counsel in that text.

Questions to Ask Yourself

1. Am I listening to the right people's opinions?
2. What do these advice givers get out of this?
3. Is this investment more beneficial for my adviser than for me?
4. What is driving my decisions? Influence? Fear? Greed? Hope? Wisdom?
5. Does my adviser have my best interests at heart?

Wisdom's To-Do List

1. Take your time and search for a reputable flat-fee broker.
2. Teach yourself to distinguish between a sales pitch and solid advice.
3. Be open to advice. There are good advisers out there.

ANCIENT ADVICE

PROVERBS 15:22—Plans fail for lack of counsel, but with many advisers they succeed.

PROVERBS 21:2—All a man's ways seem right to him. . . .

PROVERBS 26:16—The sluggard is wiser in his own eyes than seven men who answer discreetly.

PROVERBS 11:14—For lack of guidance a nation falls, but many advisers make victory sure.

PROVERBS 13:18—He who ignores discipline [instruction] comes to poverty and shame, but whoever heeds correction [counsel] is honored.

PROVERBS 13:20—He who walks with the wise grows wise, but a companion of fools suffers harm.

PROVERBS 28:26—He who trusts in himself is a fool, but he who walks in wisdom is kept safe.

V. THE GIFT

Abidan jogged along the path that led to Solomon's palace. The sky was clear of clouds and a warm breeze blew through Jerusalem. The day would turn hot long before the sun reached its zenith. Summer was not far off.

"Alms. Alms for the poor." A thin man in a dirty robe sat at the intersection of two paths, his hand held out, a hand that shook like a dry leaf on a dying tree. "Boy, help an old man. Alms for the poor."

Abidan frowned and veered around the man, avoiding the encounter and refusing to look the man in the eye.

Joy ran through Abidan like warm water. He had come to enjoy his time with the king, and the king seemed to enjoy Abidan's presence as well. To be mentored by the king was a honor that had already elevated Abidan's status among his friends.

He slowed his steps as he saw a woman with an infant in one arm attempting to gather together a stack of flax. It was not uncommon to see women with bundles of grain or flax balanced on their heads as they traveled from market to home. Others carried the day's food or water in the same fashion. This woman looked worn by a life that had just delivered another blow. She shifted the crying infant to her other arm, knelt on the hard path, and did her best to pull together what remained of the bundle before the wind blew it out of her reach. Abidan slowed as he stepped around her. It wouldn't do to be late for a meeting with the king.

Abidan arrived at the gate and was surprised to be greeted by a different servant—a young man about his age with skin several shades darker than his own and lively eyes. A few moments later, Abidan stood alone in the foyer to the great hall. Minutes passed quickly at first, then slowly, as if time were grinding to a halt.

He convinced himself that the king must be occupied with important business, affairs of state, matters concerning the Temple, or some other pressing subject.

Abidan waited. He studied the floor, the walls, the ceiling, the plaster. He listened for voices, but the great structure seemed devoid of life.

Had he come on the wrong day? Had the mentoring session been canceled? As time passed, he became more paranoid. "What have I done to offend the king?" he whispered to the empty room.

His sense of time became confused. Had he been standing alone for a few minutes or an hour? He couldn't tell. Should he stay? Should he search for someone with answers? Should he go home?

Abidan chose to wait, even if it meant standing there until the sun went down. If nothing else, it would prove how valuable he held these sessions.

The young servant appeared again and motioned for Abidan to follow. Abidan felt a breeze of relief flow through him. Finally.

Instead of being led to the courtyard, the servant directed him to the throne room. Abidan took three steps into the cavernous room then stopped midstep. The king was there, sitting on his throne and staring gravely at Abidan. Near the throne and standing to the king's left were the old beggar and the woman with the infant.

The beggar looked different. Abidan took the time to study the man's face, and what he saw chilled him. The beggar was the servant who ushered Abidan into every meeting with the king. The woman remained a stranger.

"Approach," Solomon said. Abidan heard no humor in the king's voice.

It took effort to move, as if the three pairs of eyes staring at him conspired to force him back. Abidan felt glad the child was bundled and unable to make eye contact.

Abidan crossed the short distance feeling as if he had marched a great distance. His knees felt weak, his stomach churned, and his breath came in short inhalations. "It . . . it is a pleasure to see you, O King."

"Is it?" Solomon's tone was as rough as tree bark.

Abidan could not form words.

"Tell me where you are, Abidan."

"O King, live forever, I stand before your presence in the throne room."

"You have seen me here before, is that true?"

"Yes, O King." Abidan's knees went hollow.

"What work do I accomplish here, son of Zerah?"

Abidan swallowed. "You sit as judge and counselor to those seeking your wisdom, my king."

"It is here that I arbitrate grievances, is that true?"

Abidan lowered his head, unable to face Solomon. "It is, my king."

"Tell me, Abidan, why do you suppose we meet here this morning?"

Abidan did not want to say, but he found the strength to force the words from his mouth. "These two have a grievance against me."

"They do." Solomon leaned back in the throne. He appeared weary. "You know my faithful servant. The woman is his daughter; the child, his grandson."

Abidan forced his eyes closed. He had been tested and failed. "I have disappointed, my king. I apologize."

"It is not I who deserves your apology."

"I understand." Abidan raised his head, straightened his spine, and turned to the servant and his daughter. He offered an apology. Each nodded.

The servant turned to Solomon. "With your permission, my king."

Solomon rose and stepped to the woman. He pulled back the blanket from the baby's face and smiled. "He is a handsome boy. He will make his family proud." He turned to his servant. "You may go. You have done well."

Moments later, Abidan stood alone with Solomon. He felt like a candle in an oven.

Solomon's smile disappeared with the woman and her baby. He moved to the steps that led to his throne but did not ascend. Instead, he sat on one of the stone treads. He patted the spot next to him. Abidan joined him on the steps. He waited for the harsh words that were certain to come his way.

Solomon took a deep breath, then let it out, and spoke.

> "One man gives freely, yet gains even more;
> another withholds unduly, but comes to poverty.
> A generous man will prosper;
> he who refreshes others will himself be refreshed."
>
> [Proverbs 11:24–25]

It took a moment for Abidan to realize that Solomon was not scolding him. If anything, his voice carried sadness. The king repeated the proverb. "Tell me the meaning, Abidan."

As had become their custom, Abidan repeated the proverb, then attempted an interpretation. "It means I should not have turned a blind eye to the needy."

"And what more?"

Abidan mumbled the words. "And that giving can help a man prosper."

"Does that seem right to you?"

"It seems strange to me, O King. How can a person give money away and grow richer in the process?"

"There are riches of the heart, Abidan, riches of the soul. To help others is part of the Law. Did not Moses record God's commands to help neighbors and strangers?"

"He did, O King."

"Hoarding money does not make a man wealthy, it makes him miserly. Do you know the difference?"

"Yes. I believe so. But King, I have no money. We are a poor family. I had nothing to give the beggar—I mean, your servant."

"Could you not have given him a moment of respect? Could you not have addressed him, told him that you carry no money, and blessed him in God's name?"

Abidan nodded. "Yes. I could have done that. Instead, I went out of my way to avoid him."

"And the woman with the child; did she need money?"

"No," Abidan said. "She needed help with a problem."

"But you did not offer the few minutes it would have taken to help her gather her flax and bundle it again."

"I did not want to be late, O King."

Solomon frowned. "You do me no honor by doing wrong but being punctual. I would prefer you to be late and righteous than timely and self-centered."

Abidan studied the floor again. "O King, there are so many poor. How can I help them all?"

"It is impossible for you to do so, but you can do something. You did not pass every poor person in Jerusalem. You passed two souls. Abidan, listen to me: If you cannot give of your little, you will never be able to give of your abundance. Do you understand?"

"I think so, my king."

"Building wealth is good and proper, but not if you refuse to use some of what you have to the benefit of others. There will always be poor, but such a truth does not mean the wise closes his eyes to them. Do what you can with what you have and prosperity will follow."

"Wealth is intended for the generous?"

"Yes, Abidan. Well said."

"I am sorry to have disappointed you, O King."

Solomon smiled. "Did you think it unfair of me to test you?"

Abidan shook his head. "I am not sure."

"Let me ask this: Will you forget this lesson?"

"Never, my king. I will carry this to my grave."

"Then the embarrassment you feel is worth the price."

CHAPTER 5

"GENEROSITY COUNTS TOO!"

IN A NUTSHELL: The right motive
for investment decisions

*The best investment with the least risk and the greatest
dividend is giving.*

—SIR JOHN TEMPLETON,
investor and philanthropist

The American-born British financier Sir John Templeton
knows a bit about making and using money. He also knows
something about giving it away.

Bothered that there was no Nobel Prize for religion, he founded
the Templeton Foundation Prize for the Progress of Religion.
Each year a large monetary award is given to an individual who has
contributed to the progress of religion in the world. His foundation also supports the sciences. He found giving to be a form of
investing.

What in the world does giving money away have to do with personal investing? I know you probably thought this book was about learning solid principles from one of the wisest and wealthiest men to have ever lived; about how to *increase* your wealth, not give it away. It is. In addition, I can hear you say, "I will consider the *giving* part after I have established my own net worth first." Sorry, but it doesn't work that way. Now I hear you saying, "Please don't preach that Prosperity Gospel stuff." I'm not, though I am going to share what King Solomon and other Bible writers have to say about this topic.

So tighten those safety belts and place your tray table in the closed and upright position. We are about to take off.

GROWING THROUGH GIVING

Let's start with a few words from Jesus himself. In one of His parables, Jesus said, "The King will reply, 'I tell you the truth, whatever you did for one of the least of these brothers of mine you did for me'" (Matthew 25:40). Now, granted, this statement could, and does, mean both physical and personal service, yet it also includes monetary support. There are many ways to serve those around us who may have less.

> *Earn as much as you can. Save as much as you can. Invest as much as you can. Give as much as you can.*
>
> —JOHN WESLEY,
> English evangelist and
> founder of Methodism

In this chapter we are going to focus on financial sharing. Giving of our monetary resources as well as our time and labor to those in need is rewarding, yet I hope you will also learn they are critical to your personal growth.

You have probably heard this a thousand times: "I got back so much more than I gave."

That is the focus of this chapter. It is my hope that with the help of Solomon and a few other wise men you'll come to realize how having a giving heart will help you achieve your dreams of investment success.

Let me be clear. We're not talking about a "name it and claim it" Prosperity Gospel; nor are we delving into the much misunderstood scripture of how the heavens will open to you simply because you give.

What we are going to look into is how giving helps you grow wealth. It seems counterintuitive, doesn't it? Yet it isn't. You see, making proper investments, saving for retirement, and living below your means (as we will see in the next chapter) all have something very important in common. The commonality is attitude and perspective.

> *If a person gets his attitude toward money straight, it will help straighten out almost every other area in his life.*
>
> — BILLY GRAHAM,
> American evangelist

My friend Larry, who also happens to be my accountant, attempted to teach me this very principle. He asked, "Why is more than most never enough?"

Larry has a number of wealthy, successful business clients who are always striving for more. Some of these people live in glorious homes, the type most of us see only in high-end, glossy magazines or on television shows about the ultrawealthy. Most of these people drive extremely expensive and lavish cars. They belong to country clubs, eat incredible food, and vacation in the lap of luxury. How do I know this? I used to be one of these people. Not anymore, but that's a story for another time.

I think Larry's point was, simply: When you have so much

more than most people, why subject yourself to the long hours, the acute stress, and the time spent away from the really important things in life, like your family, simply to make more money?

His thought demands answers to questions like "When is enough enough?" and "Why do you work?"

Hopefully, the answer to the first question can be found in Chapter 1, where we learned to set reasonable goals. If achieving our objectives is our goal, well, isn't that a good place to step back and possibly redirect our energy? This reasoning is only part of the answer to our questions. The remainder is, as the Apostle Paul wrote: "Work so that you may have something to give" (Ephesians 4:28).

Think about that for a moment. Work so that you might have something to give. We certainly give to our many creditors. Do these self-imposed expenses assist us in making good investment decisions? No. The money we spend to support our "quality of life" and "standard of living" does nothing but cloud our perception of what the phrase "quality of life" should mean.

As was discussed in Chapter 1, we should set goals not only for our saving targets (i.e., retirement, children's college educations), but also for objectives that help us measure our success. At what point do you have enough to live a comfortable life in order to increase your giving? (Notice I said "increase," not "start.") Giving must begin early on so your perspective remains clear and in line with your values.

Here is a hint as to how a clear, values-based perspective will enhance your ability to make quality investment decisions.

If "enough is never enough," or if you really don't know how much money it takes to live at a reasonably comfortable level, then you might be inclined to invest in questionable securities, taking risks in an attempt to maximize your investment returns.

As you can see, your personal philosophy toward investment goals, as well as financial giving, can affect your investment
decisions.

This book is not about me, but a personal story might make my
point clearer.

In Chapter 2, where I discussed goal setting, I mentioned my
use of a picture book—a book of material desires—to help moti-
vate me. I advised you to do the same. During that time of my life,
my income and investment savings went up considerably and I
achieved a hundred percent of those objectives. I can't think of that
book without feeling embarrassed by how immature it was. The
book worked.

My net worth grew and grew. I began to make business and
investment decisions I might have avoided had my situation been
different.

I was invited to invest in a start-up company that had quality
values and a terrific business plan. The company's mission was to
provide churches and other faith-based institutions, such as Chris-
tian schools and health care facilities, better access to financing in
order to assist them in meeting their goals.

Everyone involved was passionate about the company mission.
We felt we were "called" to this "Kingdom building" opportunity.
The business would be valuable to the nonprofit organizations,
while at the same time our shareholders would realize a solid
financial increase as well.

Given my extensive background in finance and investments, I
was named CEO. Now, please learn from this next piece of information: I was so excited about the values aspect of this venture *and*
about the amount of money I was being offered by the board of
directors to build this company that I lost sight of the original
motivation. Yes, I desperately wanted to help churches and schools,

but a dark cloud came as I imagined my "new" picture book of opportunities.

The company's business plan was solid, the team of professionals I put into place was magnificent, and we were attracting some of the largest banks and investors in the world. Everyone who reviewed the venture got very excited.

Our launch date came, the day we were to sign the necessary contracts that provided hundreds of millions of dollars in credit lines that we could, in turn, lend to churches, schools, and so on. It was the same day the world learned of the impending mortgage crisis in the United States and Europe. The very same day! The morning started great, then went downhill fast.

Needless to say, since this company would be in the loan business, even though we would be lending to churches and the like, our company was completely shut down before our first transaction. It's not that we didn't have customers lining up at the door, because we did. The problem was that the U.S. and European banks pulled the plug on our access to capital.

Why am I telling you this?

I invested more than $1.5 million of my own money in the company and lost 100 percent of it. I'll give you a moment to take that in. More than $1.5 million of my own money, gone. As you can imagine, my loving wife wasn't thrilled.

A SMALLER BUT BROADER PICTURE BOOK

Here is the important part of the story: I've redesigned my "picture book" of goals. Losing all that money forced me to sell all of my former attainments. The custom home—gone. The

Mercedes—gone. The fancy country club membership—gone. The world travel—gone. All of it, gone. All because I focused on "easy" riches.

My new picture book is much smaller than the first one, but it is significantly more powerful. This time, I want to see how much money I can give away. Granted, my wife and I would like to secure a retirement, as well as help our son stand on solid ground as he starts his adult life, but that's all we want for ourselves.

Believe it or not, we are happier now than at any other time in our lives. I am not saying that poverty is the goal, I'm saying that having your perspective straight as to how you want to use your money is the best. My perspective, as I have matured, is that all the personal stuff one can accumulate is really worthless. Yet to see the smile on the face of a person or ministry who is simply trying to survive and serve in this world is the greatest investment I could ever make.

This giving thing isn't new for me. I have always tried to be generous. Truth be told, I gave away a good deal of money, but only *as I lived the life of complete luxury.* How much more could I have given had I not been so greedy about my own comfort?

I hope you understand the power of this transformation. In no way am I trying to disparage your accumulation and giving standards; I am simply sharing what I have found to be true.

Our teacher Solomon taught this long ago when he wrote, "All day long he [the greedy] craves for more, but the righteous give without sparing" (Proverbs 21:26). He also taught: "One man gives freely, yet gains even more; another withholds unduly, but comes to poverty. A generous man will prosper; he who refreshes others will himself be refreshed" (Proverbs 11: 24–25).

Did God cause our new business to fail? I have no idea. Yet whether He did or not, I thank Him each day for the lessons I have come to learn and the happiness I have experienced. Am I hoping to "gain even more" by freely giving and adjusting my focus? Absolutely not! I simply want to serve His children, and not my own desires, with any gifts He chooses for me. This newfound freedom has been incredibly liberating.

I'm finding another type of riches, the kind that come from doing something for others. Trueblood's quote echoes in my mind. To plant shade trees I know I will never sit under is a noble goal. Trueblood is telling us that there is value in doing something that will help others even if it doesn't benefit us directly.

> *Nothing is more dangerous than to be blinded by prosperity.*
>
> —JOHN CALVIN,
> French theologian and reformer
>
> *A man has made at least a start on discovering the meaning of human life when he plants shade trees under which he knows full well he will never sit.*
>
> —D. ELTON TRUEBLOOD,
> American author, educator,
> philosopher, and theologian

I have heard financial "experts" advise their clients not to give until such a time that the client has accumulated and attained all his desires. "Take care of yourself first," the adviser says. "Secure your retirement, pay for your children's education, and invest your money for world travel and the luxuries you have worked so hard for."

What the adviser doesn't realize is that he is depriving his clients of one of the greatest gifts they could ever experience. In addition, the adviser is shortchanging his clients of valuable insight into goal setting and financial investment management.

At a website called Generous Giving (www.generousgiving .com), an unknown author does a good job summing up the subject of this chapter.

In essence, the author tells us that God would like us to participate in giving as a response to His gifts to us. Thus, our accountability is to God, and to no one else. No one has given us what we have but God; and we certainly will give an account to Him when we find ourselves at God's throne. The Bible is replete with verses that direct our path when it comes to giving. There may be times when we give for financial reasons that may benefit us in some way; yet, that should be a secondary concern and not the primary motivation for our gifts. Our gifts should be a response of thankfulness. The author writes:

> We should never turn off the tap of grace-inspired generosity altogether (either for tax purposes or to ensure we meet certain financial goals for our comfort and security). For God is able to meet our needs, and he is particularly pleased to do so when his children seek first his kingdom with the wealth he has entrusted them (see especially Luke 12:15–34). If a financial adviser says otherwise, well, sometimes it is appropriate to politely decline the advice of one's financial adviser.

I will even go a step further. I suggest you work with an adviser who understands that there is more to life than money. In my first book, *Demystifying Wall Street*, I spend a good deal of time discussing how to find a quality investment adviser.

Is it easier to give when you have built a large investment account? Yes. Is it easier when there is plenty of money in your bank account? Yes. Does that mean you should wait until you have attained some measure of financial comfort? Of course not.

No matter where you are on the spectrum of financial security, you should give so that you can understand the benefits of sharing and understand how, via these lessons that can be learned only in this particular way, this will help you to become a better caretaker of your money.

It is not unusual for the wealthy to give large sums of money to special needs. Joan B. Kroc, wife to the late founder of McDonald's, Ray Kroc, gave $200 million to National Public Radio; investor Warren Buffett contributed $37 billion to the Bill and Melinda Gates foundation, an organization dedicated to the eradication of malaria and river blindness.

Andrew Carnegie, the famous nineteenth-century industrialist, gave away more than $350 million in his lifetime. In today's money that would be over $4 billion. Money went to the founding of colleges, libraries, and more. He wrote, "Beyond this [$50,000, a substantial sum in the late 1800s] never earn, make no effort to increase fortune, but spend the surplus each year for benevolent purposes."

I gave large sums of money away (it's all relative), yet it never hurt to give. Looking back, the gifts may have been large in number but small in sacrifice. Does that mean it may have been a worthless gift? Certainly it was not worthless or meaningless to the recipient, but it never taught me the lessons that only sacrificial giving can teach.

You see, sacrificial giving, the kind of giving that teaches and nurtures and quite frankly blesses, was never in my purview because my sights were set on attaining more things. I would say something like, "I've given more than most, isn't that enough?" As I have said, anything given is appreciated by the recipient, but why should the less affluent giver have to miss out on the incredible benefits of sharing?

I know this is hard to hear, yet I present this to you with only sincere intentions. You see, I really want you to know how good it can feel and how much better a steward of your finances it can make you.

Here are a couple of thoughts that may help you understand the concept.

Again from the Apostle Paul: "Each man should give what he has decided in his heart to give, not reluctantly or under compulsion, for God loves a cheerful giver" (2 Corinthians 9:7).

The wonderful British writer C. S. Lewis suggested the following as a rule of thumb to determine just how much to give away: If it doesn't hurt even a little, then it is probably not enough. He writes:

> *I do not believe one can settle how much we ought to give. I am afraid the only safe rule is to give more than we can spare. In other words, if our expenditure on comforts, luxuries, amusements, etc., is up to the standard common among those with the same income as our own, we are probably giving away too little. If our charities do not at all pinch or hamper us, I should say they are too small. There ought to be things we should like to do and cannot do because our charitable expenditures exclude them.*

Remember, my intention is for you to learn to become a better investor. Some lessons are more difficult to learn than others, but I assure you, the benefits far outweigh any pain.

JUST FOR FUN . . .

It's no sin to be poor—but it's damn inconvenient.

—MARK TWAIN, author

Questions to ask Yourself

1. Do I have an idea of when enough is enough?
2. When was the last time I helped someone without thought about repayment of money or favors?
3. Can I be both frugal and giving? (The answer is yes.)
4. Do rich people give because they can, or because they care?

Wisdom's To-Do List

1. Sharing time, effort, and money with others brings an emotional wealth that lasts a lifetime.
2. Everyone needs help. Help others as you would want to be helped.
3. Healthy, robust finances are a means to higher goals. Don't lose sight of the great ideals in life.
4. You can make a difference in the lives of others. Why not do so?
5. Money is not the root of all evil, but the love of money is. Find a way to share a little of what you have.

ANCIENT ADVICE

MATTHEW 25:40—"The King will reply, 'I tell you the truth, whatever you did for one of the least of these brothers of mine, you did for me.'"

EPHESIANS 4:28—He who has been stealing must steal no longer, but must work, doing something useful with his own hands, that he may have something to share with those in need.

PROVERBS 11:24, 25—One man gives freely, yet gains even more; another withholds unduly, but comes to poverty. A generous man will prosper; he who refreshes others will himself be refreshed.

PROVERBS 21:26—All day long he craves for more, but the righteous give without sparing.

2 CORINTHIANS 9:7—Each man should give what he has decided in his heart to give, not reluctantly or under compulsion, for God loves a cheerful giver.

VI. TRULY RICH

Abidan had never ridden in a chariot before, and he found the experience exhilarating. Not only had he never been carried by chariot, he had seen very few chariots in his life. His father had explained that chariots were better suited to flat ground, not the hilly terrain around Jerusalem. Nonetheless, it was no secret that Solomon had amassed fourteen hundred such vehicles and the horses to pull them. Many were stationed in chariot cities.

The movement of the vehicle made Abidan feel as if he were flying low to the ground. The charioteer drove the horses slowly through the streets, mindful of those on foot or astride donkeys. Still, it felt as if he were moving faster than he had ever moved before.

The details of the chariot convinced Abidan that it had come from Egypt, and he assumed the horses had come from there as well. He waved at the people on the street and felt a measure of pride at being the focus of attention in his neighborhood. A dozen young children chased after them. He understood their enthusiasm.

The charioteer was a tall, thin man with a serious expression. He kept his eyes forward, occasionally shouting, "Clear the way. Clear the way!"

"*Where are we going?*" Abidan asked.

"*You shall see.*"

Abidan smiled. *He had grown used to the closed-lipped servants of the king.*

"*Will we be traveling long? I hope so.*"

"*Not long.*"

Abidan gave up questioning the driver and allowed himself to enjoy every moment that passed. The sky was clear of clouds, but smoke from cook fires tinted the air and carried the smell of baking bread and other foods.

They traveled north from the southern part of the city toward the palace. Abidan assumed Solomon had extended a kindness by providing the chariot so he would not have to cross the small city on foot as he had done each time before. That assumption faded when the driver directed the horses from the main road to a side street. Here were houses only slightly larger than the single-story dwelling in which Abidan's family of five lived.

The chariot stopped in front a plain-looking home with the typical front courtyard. "*The king awaits you inside.*"

Abided did not move. "*Our king is inside that house?*"

"*He is. Don't keep him waiting.*"

Abidan stepped down, and the chariot pulled away. Just inside the courtyard stood two stout men, each with a sword at his side. Guards, Abidan assumed.

He opened the simple gate in the wall and entered the courtyard. He took a few steps toward the closest man. "*I am Abidan, son of Zerah. I am to meet with the king.*" *His voice wavered as he stood in the man's large shadow.*

"*In there,*" *the guard said, pointing to the door of the home. Abidan inhaled deeply and started for the door, which stood open, no doubt to let in the morning breeze. He crossed the threshold. As with most houses in*

Jerusalem, the interior was divided into functional units: a sleeping area, a food preparation area, and a sitting area. King Solomon reclined at a long, smooth table, propping himself up on his right arm and taking food from bowls with his left hand. An old man with drawn features and white hair reclined on a dining bench opposite the king. Abidan assumed him to be the owner.

Solomon looked up. "Abidan, I see you have arrived safely. Did you enjoy your journey here?"

"Yes, O King, may you live forever. You did a great favor to me by sending the chariot."

"Not at all, Abidan. It was easier than sending a messenger with directions. Besides, a young man of your age still enjoys such things."

"I hope that someday I can own such a fine chariot."

Solomon tilted his head. "Do you?" He looked at the old man and raised an eyebrow. The old man smiled but said nothing. "Well, for now, come and join us. Nemuel has set a table for us."

Abidan moved to another bench and joined them around the table. A bowl of dates, dried fish, and several loaves of bread rested on the table. Nemuel sat up and poured water mixed with wine into Abidan's cup. Abidan thanked him.

"This is the boy you have been telling me about?" Nemuel said. "He looks smart."

Solomon laughed. "He looks confused." To Abidan he said, "Are you confused, son?"

"Yes, my king. I assumed I would be taken to your palace."

"Even kings must leave the confines of their home from time to time. I wanted to visit with my friend in his palace."

Abidan stifled the urge to laugh. Certainly the home was larger than his and he could see that it held several fine things, but it was no palace.

"I am honored to be here."

"He is polite, too," Nemuel said with a smile. Abidan could see that several teeth were missing. Not unusual in a man his age.

"As a young man, Nemuel served in my father's court and provided sound advice and wisdom. I came to know him when I was close to your age, Abidan. We became friends. After I became king, he served me for several years."

"But no longer?" Abidan asked.

"He has taken his leisure. I come by for conversation and advice from time to time."

Abidan took a date and bit into it. He studied Nemuel for a moment, then the king. He had experienced enough lessons with the king to know the sovereign often started the lesson before Abidan realized it.

"To serve the king must be an honor," Abidan said.

"It was. I take pride in the work I did."

The conversation shifted to Nemuel's recollections of Solomon's father, King David, and the constant intrigue that surrounded him. Abidan said little, waiting for the moment when the king would put him on the spot with some question. Time passed and finally Solomon rose from the bench and took his leave. Abidan followed the king from the house, still confused as to why he had been invited to join them around the table.

"Let us walk back to the palace," Solomon said.

"Walk?"

"I enjoy walking and you are still young, so it shall be no strain on you."

"Yes, O King. Of course."

As they exited the courtyard and turned north, the two guards in the courtyard walked a short distance behind them. Two other guards, men Abidan had not seen when he arrived, walked ten paces ahead. The charioteer followed behind them all.

"How does it feel to have shared a meal with one of the richest men *in Jerusalem?" Solomon placed his hands behind his back, and bowed his head slightly like a man deep in thought.*

"I value every minute I am privileged to spend with you, O King."

Solomon shook his head. "I was not referring to me."

Abidan's mind tripped over the words. "I'm sorry, O King, I do not understand. Who are you speaking of?"

"Nemuel, of course. There were only three of us at the table, Abidan."

"I know . . . I only meant . . . Nemuel is a wealthy man?"

"One of the wealthiest you shall ever meet." Solomon paused and studied Abidan's face. "You look puzzled."

"I am, my king. I mean, his house is nice, but not the kind of home rich people build for themselves. It is only slightly larger than my father's, and we are not wealthy."

"You count wealth by the size of a man's home?"

Abidan felt as if he had just stepped onto a slippery slope. "No, O King."

"Then how does one recognize a wealthy person?"

Abidan tried to tread carefully and was slow in responding.

Solomon prompted him. "Abidan, sometimes it is best to speak honestly rather than searching for the answer you think I want."

"Yes, O King. Wealthy people wear fine clothes, have big homes, own things the rest of us can't."

"It is true that many do as you say, yet Nemuel is very wealthy but he does not spend his wealth on a large home and expensive clothing."

"But why, O King? If he can afford these things, why does he not buy them?"

Solomon raised his head, took a deep breath, then said, "One man pretends to be rich yet has nothing; another pretends to be poor yet has great wealth" [Proverbs 13:7]. The king said nothing more. There was no need. Abidan had been down the teaching road before.

As always, Abidan recited the words several times, committing them to memory. "Nemuel pretends to be poor but is wealthy?"

"Close, Abidan. As you said, his house is larger than yours. He lives in one of the better parts of the city, close to the Temple and other public buildings. He can afford a great deal more, but he chooses the lifestyle you saw."

"O King, may I ask a question?"

"Please do."

"If your friend is wealthy but he worked in your father's court, then how did he come by his wealth? Did he inherit his money?"

"No, and I shall save you the trouble of asking. I did not give him wealth."

"I do not understand, my king."

"Few people do, Abidan. Nemuel has spent his life managing his money. He can afford a more expensive house but the one he has meets the needs of he and his family. He can buy the finest foods, but simple food has kept him full and well. What money he did not spend, he saved for his future. Abidan, do you know many men Nemuel's age who live as he does?"

Abidan searched his memory. "No, King. Most men work until they die or can work no longer. If they cannot work, then their families support them."

"Nemuel no longer works and he takes care of himself and his wife. He can do this because he thought it better to spend only what he needed to spend, not what he could spend. Do you understand?"

"I am trying to understand, O King. Nemuel lives in comfort because he was not careless with his money. He thought of the future, not of the moment."

"You have said it well, Abidan. Now what is the lesson for you?"

"I should spend money on my needs, not my wants. Over time I will amass enough savings for future needs."

"Exactly."

"But, O King . . ." Abidan could not bring himself to ask the question.

"I did not hear all of your words."

"It is nothing, O King. My question is improper."

"You want to know why, if my words are wise, that I live in such a large palace and wear such fine clothing, have so many servants, and live in luxury. Is that your question?"

Abidan lowered his head. "Yes, O King."

"There are many reasons. First, my wealth has grown so much that I cannot spend it all. It will pass on to my heirs and the kingdom after my death. Two, I am the king of the whole land. My influence extends from Egypt in the south to the great Euphrates River. I represent not only myself but the whole kingdom. I deal with kings of many countries. It is important that they see me as a person of power, strength, wealth, and wisdom."

"I see."

"My situation is unique. What Nemuel has done, anyone can do."

Abidan nodded. "One man pretends to be rich yet has nothing; another pretends to be poor yet has great wealth." He thought about the words some more. "There are those who appear rich but are in reality poor. There are those who others judge to be poor, but are really rich."

"Yes, Abidan. In both cases, the rich and the poor have made a choice. You will face the same choice."

"I will make the correct one, O King."

"I am certain you will."

CHAPTER 6

"LIVE BELOW YOUR MEANS"

IN A NUTSHELL: Find and create the money to invest.

Thousands upon thousands are yearly brought into a state of real poverty by their great anxiety not to be thought poor.

—WILLIAM CORBETT,
English composer

Please don't skip this chapter. I even considered titling this section something else, like "Enjoying Extra Money in the Bank" or "You Have Nothing to Prove to Anyone," anything to get you to read this part of the book. Yet honesty prevailed, and we are stuck with the simple fact that the people who end up with the most money in the bank tend to be those whom you would never think of as wealthy. Some may call them tightwads; I call them wise.

Now, if you think this is going to be the hardest chapter for you to read, I want you to know it was the hardest for me to write. You see, I am one of those William Corbett spoke of, even though I wasn't born until a couple of hundred years after he uttered those words. I have learned a great deal about this subject, and I desperately want you to learn them as well. Thus I will be using a good number of very personal stories. I am willing to share my many faults to help you avoid the mistakes I made and the traps I fell into.

I am often asked, "How do I get the extra money to pay off debt and invest?" The answer isn't always easy to hear: Spend less, don't buy things unless you truly need them, learn to live below your means.

Let's be honest: that kind of thinking isn't part of our culture. We are a people of immediate gratification. We know what we want, how we want it, and we want it now. That attitude has become a hallmark of every generation since the baby boomers. Please understand, I'm not preaching here. For much of my life I have been a card-carrying member of the "I want it and I want it now" club. The credit card industry has experienced explosive growth because so many of us have this attitude.

Nonetheless, the number of people who have created wealth through frugality is too large to count. It amazes many to learn how frugal some rich people are.

THE PROBLEM OF STARTING

When you were young and making only $15,000 per year, you were probably confident that when you got a better, higher-paying job, you would be in a position to save some money. You finally got the job. Did you save more? No, you bought a car that would run reliably and rationalized the purchase by saying you couldn't afford to lose this good job because of car trouble. That makes sense.

Now you are making $25,000 annually, and because of the car payments and the money you are spending going out with your friends, which you can do because you are making more money, you don't have anything left to save. That's okay; you have been assured a promotion sometime in the near future. With it will come a raise, which, you tell yourself, will allow you to begin saving for the future. No problem, you're still young.

The promotion comes, just as you knew it would, given your work ethic and dedication to your job. Congratulations! Wow, now you are making $40,000 a year. This huge increase will surely allow you to start putting money away for your future. Just as your income starts to grow, you meet the person of your dreams. She is perfect and the two of you decide to marry the following summer.

Courting her may have been expensive, but boy, it was worth it. You wanted to treat her to better restaurants, concerts, and some of the nicer things in life. The two of you work hard at your jobs and deserve to have fun times. You say, "All work and no play . . ."

Now you're married. Now you're buying your first house. Of course the house needs furniture. Before long you need a minivan for the kids.

Do you see how far we can go with this story? We could easily move all the way through life's changes, right up to retirement. I understand. I've been there. I climbed through the income strata until I reached incredible levels, but always had some good reason not to save. I can assure you that with every increase in income there comes a nicer home, finer cars, more lavish vacations, a country club membership, newer clothes, finer restaurants, private schools, travel, and a thousand other desires hungry for your cash. You feel that you can afford it, so why not?

WHY WE DON'T SAVE

The problem of not saving has two main parts. The first is simply that as we age and move through the normal life stages there are more and more things to spend money on. All of this is true yet there is another force, a powerful, suggestive, manipulative force beckoning us to spend more money and reach higher levels of enjoyment.

This force has a name: Madison Avenue. If you are not aware, this is the place where many commercials, designed to make us spend more money, are made. These people are incredibly smart. They have a keen understanding of human behavior and could have taught Sigmund Freud and Carl Jung a few things. In a nutshell, they know what makes us buy things we don't need, don't want, can't afford, and otherwise aren't worth the price. These people are masters of emotional responsiveness. Let's just say they play to win, and win they do.

These marketers have an astonishing talent for "helping" us realize how much happier we could be if only we had . . . How much better life would be if we owned . . . How much more people would like us if only . . . How much more successful we could be if we did . . . You get the picture. If you think you can consistently avoid these subtle, and often not so subtle, messages, you may be fooling yourself. Billions and billions of dollars are spent each year

THE SOLOMON SECRET | 113

on advertising. If it didn't work, manufactures of products wouldn't spend this money. Someone is buying all this stuff.

There have been several studies that show today's consumer receives up to three thousand marketing messages a day. Low estimates are 850 to 1,000 messages a day. Whatever the actual number, we are bombarded with messages about product. Some come via television, others by radio, Internet, e-mail, billboards, direct mail, and more. No wonder it seems like such a natural reflex.

The second part of the problem of spending more than we save is our own attitude toward money. Many believe they can buy happiness. It sounds silly when we say it, and we all deny it, but our actions say the opposite.

Why do we constantly fall for this lie? Because life is hard and we long to be like the smiling, healthy, fit, beautiful people we see in commercials. They look like their lives are perfect. Who wouldn't want to be like

> *He who is not contented with what he has will not be contented with what he doesn't have.*
>
> —SOCRATES,
> Greek philosopher

them? Why is it we never see an overweight, depressed guy with bags under his eyes from working many long hours, and sleeping poorly because of unrelenting financial worries, on these commercials?

In addition to that, we rightly or wrongly believe we deserve all these nice things. We work hard and deserve some enjoyment. I couldn't agree more—though, with a twist.

When I was a "rich" guy, I used to buy the most expensive of everything I desired, be it TVs, cars, homes, food, clothes, jewelry, furniture, etc. You get the picture? I was held captive by the foolish and false assumption that if it cost more, it must be worth more. I imagined the manufacturer couldn't get away with charging more if the item wasn't of considerably higher quality. What a fool I was.

Let me give you a few personal examples.

Jeans. Yes, a simple pair of jeans. I used to spend eighty-five dollars on designer jeans from Nordstrom. (There was a time I bought almost everything in my wardrobe from Nordstrom. After all, they had a guy playing piano right in the middle of the store.) I went through pairs and pairs of those expensive jeans because they never quite fit right, so I would buy a different pair, hoping for a better fit.

As I write this, I am wearing my favorite jeans. These are the most comfortable, longest-lasting, best-fitting jeans I have *ever* owned. And by the way, they cost a whopping eight dollars at Wal-Mart.

No piano player, no perfume-scented aisles, no perfectly manicured and sickeningly sweet sales associates, and no mannequins that look better than anyone I've ever met. Just great jeans for eight bucks.

Want more? I used to drive a Mercedes, a Lexus, and other very expensive cars. They were fun to drive. The problem was, I always worried that some dumb driver, probably in an old, cheap car, would damage my shiny, flashy, sexy, expensive ride. I could never relax and just enjoy my car. In addition, whenever I took the car in for service, it cost me hundreds of dollars.

Now, in my new state of elderly wisdom, I drive cars that get beat up from road conditions around where I live. In the mountains, we have snowstorms that cover rocks, poles, and other assorted items lying in wait for someone to drive by. We also suffer broken windshields from the stuff they place on our roads to assist cars with traction. In addition, we have off-road trails that can transport you to some of the most incredible views you will ever see. What a joy it is to not care who is looking at your car, to get scratches, dings, and dents and not even notice. Now when I take my car to get it serviced, I sit around with the mechanic and drink coffee while talking about the upcoming ski season. It's pure joy.

SIMPLE WAYS TO SAVE MONEY

Food. I used to frequent the finest restaurants. When I would walk into one of these establishments, the maître d' would welcome me by name. The lovely, model-like hostess would walk my guests and me to a prominent table. After seating us she would gracefully unfold our linen napkins and place them gently on our laps. When the food was delivered, by the necessary number of waiters in order that all of the dishes were uncovered at once, the servers would wish us "bon appétit" and then leave. I found it most beneficial to my ego.

It all seems a bit excessive now, but I must admit, it was pretty cool then. Cool or not, it proved to be a waste of money. Here's what I've found: I am just as full after eating Taco Bell for five dollars as I am after eating at an expensive restaurant and dropping a hundred dollars. Quite the revelation, isn't it?

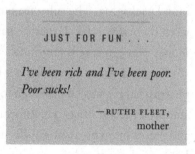

JUST FOR FUN . . .

I've been rich and I've been poor. Poor sucks!

—RUTHE FLEET,
mother

Please understand, I am not saying you shouldn't enjoy life, or spend money to acquire valuable things. I am saying that we need to adjust our thinking about how we spend money and the effects it has on our future. Just remember, more expensive does not necessarily mean better.

Let me give you a few examples from the grocery industry.

First of all, always use the store's savings card. I don't know of any card that actually costs money to obtain, and you can save significant amounts of money by using it. Grocery stores generally "red tag" items that save the shopper money. The store is trying to help you be frugal. If you don't use these cards every time you do your grocery shopping then you are throwing money in the trash. It's as simple as that.

In addition to the store savings card, always review the coupons available in your local newspaper. The grocery manager who graciously helped me gather this information stated that with the combination of coupons and the store's savings card, customers can save as much as 80 percent off the listed price—80 percent.

This store manager also suggested that a customer generally should focus on store brands over name-brand products. The store brand is always cheaper, usually of similar quality, and many times even made by the name-brand companies and placed in the store-brand packaging. The rules are simple and the stores will help you learn them if you ask. It may be hard to believe, but the amount of money you can save is enormous.

Finally, I spent time talking with a friend who is a registered pharmacist. He was kind enough to talk with me about both generic and prescription drugs. He informed me that generic medications and prescription meds are equally governed and standardized by the FDA. Generic brands are just as good as the name-brand drugs.

It was in the over-the-counter aisle that I really became fascinated. For almost every product I noticed a store brand. What I found was that for the store brand, the active ingredients are 99.9 percent similar to the brand name. Sometimes, when on the store-brand package it states "compare to" this or that specific brand product, the requirements are that the store brand must be virtually identical. The store must even file an application with the FDA in order to use the "compare to" message on the label of its product.

Let's take a look at some savings I found simply by looking around the shelf.

Advil 200 mg ibuprofen, fifty tablets, sold for $8.49 in this particular store. Directly next to Advil on the shelf was the Safeway brand, fifty tablets of 200 mg ibuprofen for $4.79. That is almost 44 percent off. In addition, I found on the Safeway label the letters USP, and inquired as to their meaning. I assumed they must be important, as they were prominently displayed on the front of the label.

I learned that USP means the product has met the United States Pharmacopeia standard. The following comes directly from the USP website:

The United States Pharmacopeia (USP) is an official public standards–setting authority for all prescription and over-the-counter medicines and other health care products manufactured or sold in the United States. USP also sets widely recognized standards for food ingredients and dietary supplements. USP sets standards for the quality, purity, strength, and consistency of these products—critical to the public health. USP's standards are recognized and used in more than

130 countries around the globe. These standards have helped to ensure public health throughout the world for close to 200 years.

This seems to mean that the store brand has met the same standards as the name brand.

You may even find the letters USP on vitamins and herbal supplements. Now that I know the significance of these three letters, I will always favor a store product that has them on the label, and at the same time will save significant amounts of money.

Here is another example:

Many people use glucosamine products for their creaky joints. I noticed the Schiff product called Move Free Advanced Triple Strength glucosamine and chondroitin. The price for the eighty-tablet bottle, 1,500 mg, was $32.39. On the shelf directly below was Safeway Advanced Triple Strength 1,500 mg glucosamine and chondroitin, an eighty-tablet bottle, for $11.98—and you got a second bottle free. Friends, that's a 63 percent savings.

Now, I am in no way trying to beat up on name-brand products. I'm also not endorsing Safeway; this store is simply where I happen to shop. With that said, my simple research into pricing at grocery stores has certainly changed my personal habits.

Finally, as I looked throughout the store, I found that almost every product, right on down to bathroom tissue, had a far less expensive alternative. I don't know about yours, but my rear end can't tell the difference.

You see, I will never suggest that you should forgo purchasing things that you need, or even those things that you simply desire. What I want you to understand is that you can save a significant amount of money by purchasing smart. With that money you can lower your debt, or invest.

PRIDE GOETH BEFORE THE FALL

I have heard people say that when they use coupons or shop at discounters like Wal-Mart, they feel people will view them as poor, or even worse, cheap. You need to get over that right now. Most rich people would view you as smart because they shop the same way. Product sellers laugh at those who think it is beneath them to practice frugal shopping, and they are laughing all the way to the bank. They know they can offer fantastic discounts because there are many who won't take advantage of the savings, all because of pride.

Don't just take my word for it. If you need extra motivation to act in a similar way as the *truly* wealthy, then read the book *The Millionaire Next Door*, by Thomas Stanley and William Danko. Here are a couple of thoughts from that book: "The opposite of frugal is wasteful. We define wasteful as a lifestyle marked by lavish spending and hyper-consumption. Being frugal is the cornerstone of wealth-building."

The authors go on with this thought: "Wealth is more often the result of a lifestyle of hard work, perseverance, planning and most of all, self-discipline. They become millionaires by budgeting and controlling expenses, and they maintain their affluent status the same way."

Are you getting the point? If you are willing to reconsider your purchasing habits, and get rid of some of your pride, you will be practicing the methods of the truly wealthy. Many, however, mimic the patterns of those who strive to appear rich while hiding their financial struggles.

Which group do you think Solomon might choose to "hang" with? Think about his words written in Proverbs 13:7: "One man

> *I finally know what distinguishes man from the other beasts: financial worries.*
>
> —JULES RENARD,
> French writer

pretends to be rich yet has nothing; another pretends to be poor yet has great wealth."

I would contend that the one who pretends to be rich does, in fact, have something to show for his troubles—a lot of debt!

WHEN IT COMES TO MONEY, SAVING BRINGS GREATER HAPPINESS

It has taken me a good amount of time to learn that spending money does not lead to happiness, but having considerable "unspent" money in the bank leads to contentment.

I have found that people who are willing to release themselves from the manipulation of pricing and the Madison Avenue machine tend to be far more content.

I can tell you my wife and I are so much happier since we removed ourselves from the treadmill. Life is easier, more enjoyable, and definitely less stressful. Friends are real, not simply hanging around because they want us to spend money on them.

And, of course, we must ask what we are teaching our children when we practice wasteful spending.

Here are a few more quotations that I like on this subject. I hope they will inspire you.

Millionaires seldom smile.

—ANDREW CARNEGIE,
American industrialist and philanthropist

I was happier when I was doing a mechanic's job.

—HENRY FORD,
American industrialist

I have made many millions, but they have brought me no happiness.

—JOHN D. ROCKEFELLER SR.,
American industrialist and philanthropist

So put these ideas to work for you. Follow the wisdom of the richest man to have ever lived. Stop foolishly spending and start saving and investing.

Questions to Ask Yourself

1. Do I spend more money than I should on things I don't really need?
2. Am I living above my means instead of below?
3. Do I have more unnecessary debt this year than last year?
4. Small changes make a difference, so where can I spend less?
5. Am I letting advertising and marketing pick my pocket?

Wisdom's To-Do List

1. Survey your spending habits. You don't have to live like a monk, but there is no need to throw money away.

2. Make a commitment to spend less on frivolous things and use the money to advance your life.

3. Don't be addicted to spending. There are many things in life that bring happiness and many of them are free.

ANCIENT ADVICE

PROVERBS 13:7—One man pretends to be rich yet has nothing; another pretends to be poor yet has great wealth.

PROVERBS 11:28—Whoever trusts in his riches will fall, but the righteous will thrive like a green leaf.

VII. A KINGLY VISIT

Abidan's back hurt. His wrists hurt more. The repetitive motion of moving the bow string over the awl while applying pressure to the top of the pointed tool took its toll. Sweat dripped from his forehead and fell on the curved segment of wood destined to be part of a spoke wagon wheel. Harder still was facing the truth that he had four more sections in which to drill holes for the spokes. His father bent over the rough and crude bench, shaving and trimming the pieces so they would fit together.

The thick, dusty air in the small shop made things worse, but Abidan refused to complain. This was his life. His father was a carpenter, and his father before him. His life would be surrounded by wood and hard work. Still, working in the shop was better than the work they'd done last week. For three days, he and his father set roof beams on stone walls for a new house. Outside work was often more enjoyable, but when the sun reached midday, it sapped him of his strength. He had no idea how his father continued.

He took a deep breath and blew the loose shavings from the freshly bored hole, then he noticed the sound of sandals scuffing on the stone stoop at the door—like the arrival of several people. It was too early for the midday meal. His mother wouldn't bring food for another hour.

Abidan turned, still holding the tools in his hands.

King Solomon stood at the door.

"My king," Abidan's father said, and bowed slightly.

Solomon laughed, stepped into the dirty shop, and embraced his friend. "It has been too long, Zerah."

Zerah returned the embrace. "It has, my king. The hours too quickly become months."

Abidan shuddered. The king stood in their humble shop, a simple stone-and-mud enclosure with a leaky roof. It was this way with all carpenters whose days were spent laboring for others, leaving them little time to care for their own homes and businesses.

"Abidan!" Solomon said. His voice filled the space.

"My king." Abidan set the tools down and approached. "I did not know you were coming." He felt embarrassed by his dirty, sweat-stained clothing.

"You have come to the palace so many times, I thought it right to come to you. Besides, I have not seen your father for so long. I am afraid I have behaved improperly and neglected my friend."

"No, my king," Zerah said. "You have done more for me than a man of my position has a right to ask. Your work with Abidan has been re-markable. Over the last few weeks he insists on rising before me and coming to the shop early. He also stays late, long after others in the area have quit."

"Is this so, Abidan?"

"Yes, O King. I am trying to be diligent as you have taught."

The king nodded, but Abidan detected a sadness in him. Solomon turned to Zerah. "I have brought food and drink to share a meal with your family."

"You are too kind, my king."

Solomon smiled. "I have brought enough for your neighbors as well. Can you spare the time to feast with us?"

"Of course, my king." Zerah's smile almost touched his ears. "You honor my house and family."

"The pleasure is mine, my friend. Will you please show my servants to your home? They will take care of everything."

"Yes, O King." Zerah was out the door a moment later.

"And you, Abidan, will you join us?"

Abidan was conflicted. "My work is not yet done, O King."

"I see." He sighed. "I have one more lesson for you, Abidan. I see that I have not arrived too soon."

"I do not understand."

Solomon moved a few hand tools from the low bench and leaned against it.

"I will get a chair for you—"

"No. I am fine."

Abidan's face warmed.

Solomon laughed. "What embarrasses you, Abidan?"

"The dirt of our shop, O King. You deserve much better. Had I known you were coming, I could have made preparations."

"Abidan, never feel shame over your work or the place you do it. This shop does not offend me. I admire the work that goes on here."

"Thank . . . thank you, my king."

"I have done a disservice to you, son."

"What? Oh no, my king. You have shared your wisdom with me. I am a better person for it."

"Wisdom comes in steps. Is it true that you work longer than your father?"

"Yes. I have encouraged my father to take more assignments."

Solomon nodded. "Think on this saying: 'Do not wear yourself out to get rich; have the wisdom to show restraint'" [Proverbs 23:4].

Abidan did not have to decipher the meaning. Of all the proverbs Solomon had shared with him, this was the clearest and the most convicting. Still, he repeated the proverb several times.

"Your face tells me you understand the meaning," Solomon said.

"I do, my king."

"Tell me the truth of it."

Abidan took a deep breath. "It means it is not wise to pursue riches."

"No, son. You are wrong. It is not the pursuit of riches that is wrong."

"Then what, O King?"

"You tell me, Abidan."

Abidan brushed flecks of wood from his forearms and uttered the last part of the proverb. ". . . have the wisdom to show restraint. Restraint. Wisdom to show restraint . . ." He shook his head, and then an idea occurred to him. "There is a balance between striving for riches and restraint."

Solomon smiled. "Meaning?"

Abidan frowned. "It makes no sense to me, my king. Why would a man restrain himself in the pursuit of riches?"

"To live, Abidan. To live."

"To live?"

"To gain riches is wise; to pay for riches with happiness is foolishness." Solomon stood and began to pace. "Everything comes at a price, Abidan, does it not? To arrive early at your father's shop requires that you pay by sleeping less. I see you and your father are working on wagon wheels."

"Yes," Abidan said with pride. "We have several more to make. It is the most wagon wheels we have made for one customer. I found the customer."

"You are to be praised, Abidan. Has that changed things?"

"It has. The money will help my family and build our business."

"Does you mother love wagon wheels?"

The question caught Abidan off guard. "No, my king."

"Does she love you?"

"Yes."

"Would she trade you for wagon wheels?"

Abidan straightened. "Of course not, my king."

"Then do not trade her for fast riches."

The words stung. "I am not—"

"You are not what, Abidan?"

Abidan lowered his head.

"When I was a young man, Abidan, I used to be impatient when I traveled. I always wanted to be at the destination. It took me some time to learn the journey is often more interesting than the destination. Do you understand?"

Abidan nodded. "I should learn to enjoy the journey and not just think of the destination."

"Exactly so, Abidan. Work hard. Make your riches, but enjoy those around you. Enjoy your family. Spent days can never be recaptured. Build your father's business and when it becomes your business, build it some more, but know when to show restraint. Enjoy the day. Enjoy the work. Enjoy the journey. Choose contentment for today but think on the future."

"Yes, my king."

"Now, I ask again. Will you join us for the feast?"

Abidan glanced at his tools and gazed at the wood he had been working on. It would be there tomorrow, he decided. The best work he could do now was spend time with his king, his family, and his neighbors. "Yes, my king. I will enjoy a feast with you."

"Good. Maybe I'll tell you stories about your father."

Abidan laughed. "I do have one question, O King."

"Ask it."

"Is it true that you have a thousand wives and concubines?"

"It is true. Most are political marriages."

"What is it like to have so many wives?

"Oh, Abidan, you do not want to know."

CHAPTER 7

"SLOW AND STEADY"

IN A NUTSHELL: It's all about pacing.

Never spend your money before you have it.

—THOMAS JEFFERSON,
author of the Declaration of Independence
and third president of the United States

Here's the cold, hard truth: Unless you get really lucky, or you have a rich uncle who likes you the best and dies, it takes a long time to accumulate a lot of money.

If you view this fact as a reason to give up or simply not try, you will miss some of the greatest lessons life has to offer. The lessons are learned in the journey, not in the destination. Throughout this book, Solomon has shared with us nuggets of gold, riches of his wisdom, and given us an understanding of the treasures in life we can accumulate *while* on the path to wealth.

TOO RICH TOO FAST?

There are many stories of instant millionaires whose lives were ruined by sudden wealth; ordinary people who won the lottery or came into big money with an "overnight" success only to find themselves with severe problems a few years later. Unfortunately, such accounts are a dime a dozen.

Consider child stars whose lives were distorted by wealth at an early age. I would suggest that these people lost their childhoods because they gained too much success and too much money too early. Michael Jackson, Lindsay Lohan, Macaulay Culkin, Danny Bonaduce, Tatum O'Neal, Judy Garland, and so many others lacked the maturity that comes with age and experience.

There are people of extraordinary talent who endure hardship in their lives, in large part, because they couldn't handle success, and spent their money on destructive practices. Think of John Belushi, the actor and brilliant comedian who died of an overdose of cocaine and heroin at just thirty-three years of age. Chris Farley, thirty-three, died of a cocaine and heroin overdose complicated by obesity. Jim Morrison, twenty-seven, lead singer for the rock group The Doors, died of a heart attack due to possible drug overdose. Twenty-seven-year-old musician and stellar guitarist Jimi Hendrix died from an overdose of sleeping pills. At just thirty-six, actress Marilyn Monroe died of a drug overdose.

Some might argue that these are examples of drug-using, spoiled brats who had everything and still couldn't be happy. In some cases, that may be true. A more compassionate and honest way to view these people is to remember that many of these talented individuals were regular, hardworking folks who were passionate about being recognized for their talent. Unfortunately, the recognition came too fast and too soon. Certainly many factors contributed to their self-destructive behavior, but it would be difficult to deny the impact of sudden wealth, wealth obtained before wisdom.

It takes time to mature. It takes time to season. It takes time to develop an appreciation for the meaning of life. Only then can we be grateful for, and see with mature eyes, the rewards of our hard work and savings.

As we noted before, Solomon said, "The plans of the diligent lead to profit as surely as haste leads to poverty" (Proverbs 21:5). Isn't that the point of the stories above? When money comes too hastily, it almost always leads to some form of poverty, if not financial, then emotional, social, or spiritual. I imagine that most of my readers are old enough to know that self-destructive behavior is the symptom, not the disease.

Facts are facts. It takes years and even decades to grow your wealth wisely.

THE POWER OF PERSPECTIVE

Thomas Jefferson, one of our wisest founding fathers, stated, "Never spend your money before you have it." This is excellent advice, yet so many ignore this truth. Day after day they use their credit cards to make purchases with the intent of paying for them later. Why? Because they, like most of us, are part of the immediate gratification generation. We want it now, and credit cards allow us to have it. Jefferson would be appalled.

I believe that one of the reasons we are in such a rush to accumulate wealth, which we believe will in turn provide for a better life, is that we are discontented with our current existence. Why is that? If you are reading this and are living in the developed world, you are already enjoying a better, more comfortable, easier life than most of the world. We have a propensity to forget, on a daily basis, how lucky we are even without a lot of money.

I'm just like everyone else. I face the same temptations, harbor the same desires, have big dreams, want nice things, and occasionally feel that I deserve more than I have. When these thoughts percolate to the top of my mind, I remind myself of several things. In the next twenty-four hours, approximately thirty thousand people, mostly children, will die of starvation. Thirty thousand! Over a billion people have no access to safe water. In some parts of the world, any home over five hundred square feet is considered a mansion. Ninety-five percent of humanity lives on less than ten dollars a day.

Please understand, I'm not trying to make anyone feel bad about the wealth they have. Wealth is a great tool to right wrongs, correct social ills, and more. I'm just trying to help myself and you maintain perspective.

In no way am I suggesting that we shouldn't save, invest, or try to accumulate more money. After all, that's what this book is about. I *am* suggesting that if we are genuinely content with our current position in life and maintain a comfortable level of existence in each stage of life, we will make better decisions about saving and investing.

This attitude of contentment and financial responsibility is

> It's never too early to teach your children about the tool of money. Teach them how to work for it and they learn pride and self-respect. Teach them how to save it and they learn security and self-worth. Teach them how to be generous with it and they learn love.
>
> —JUDITH JAMISON,
> African-American dancer
> and choreographer

one of the greatest lessons we can teach our children. Imagine the blessing for our children as they learn, by our example, to be happy no matter their current financial circumstances. And along with this, we could teach them to be good managers of their money in order to responsibly save and invest for their future.

The Apostle Paul wrote a wonderful verse on this very topic. He said, "I know what it is to be in need, and I know what it is to have plenty. I have learned the secret of being content in any and every situation, whether well fed or hungry, whether living in plenty or in want" (Philippians 4:12).

I hope you find "peace" in all circumstances. I can assure you that your life will be happier if you can practice this truth.

A pastor friend of mine, Eric, delivered a Sunday sermon on the fruit of the spirit (Galatians 5:22–23) in a way I had never heard before. Stay with me as I try to recapture his explanation.

PLEASE PASS THE MANURE

Eric reminded us that one of the "fruits" of the spirit is joy. Everyone was comfortable with this, as we had all read at least portions of the Bible and knew this to be true. He moved on to compare the spirit to soil, as fruit is one of the wondrous products to spring forth from the ground. Eric walked us through the idea that the "richer" the soil, the juicer, the bigger, the tastier the fruit.

I was with him so far even though I had no idea where he was headed with this analogy.

He then went on to ask the obvious question. Eric said, "If we accept that better fruit comes forth from richer soil, then what is it that makes soil rich?" His answer and terminology generated a reaction from the congregation, in the form of both laughter and a bit of shock. He went on to remind us that it is "crap" or a more politically correct term, "manure," that makes soil rich.

Now I was completely lost, but I had faith in my friend. I stayed with him hoping for an understandable punch line.

Eric suggested that there will be crap in our lives. That's to be expected. Then he put a positive spin on it. Crap is exactly what we need to enrich our spirit, and a richer spirit would in turn produce more joy. He gave me something to think about.

The concept took root in my mind. It started to make sense to me that the difficult times in our lives—more than the good times—grow the most important character traits in us. This impression stayed with me and had a profound impact on my reaction to all the crap that was taking place in my life. I now welcomed the manure knowing that it would produce better fruit (more love, joy, peace, patience, kindness, goodness, faithfulness, gentleness, and self-control).

So what is my point? It is this: Be happy with where you are while saving and investing for your future. Don't wait until you're rich to be happy. It's a waste of life. Enjoy today while planning for tomorrow.

> *Patience and perseverance have a magical effect before which difficulties disappear and obstacles vanish.*
>
> —JOHN QUINCY ADAMS, sixth president of the United States and son of the second president, John Adams

King Solomon was certainly aware of this. He taught us, "A faithful man will be richly blessed, but one eager to get rich will not go unpunished" (Proverbs 28:20). What did he mean by "faithful"? I believe he meant one who is content in his current position while working hard on his future.

Slow and steady wins the race. It's an old chestnut, but an accurate one.

THE TRIP IS AS IMPORTANT
AS THE DESTINATION

There are hundreds of stories of people who worked ordinary jobs and had minimal incomes throughout their lives. They lived in a manner that was commensurate with their income. They seemed happy, raised their children to appreciate the simple things in life, and flew the flag on the Fourth of July. These folks were always seen at the local picnics, fireworks shows, and town parades. They could be counted on to volunteer when needed, to bake a pie for local events, and not miss many days of work.

They sound like millions of Americans, yet there is one thing they did differently from the rest of us. They saved and invested a small amount of money from *every* paycheck. Their names are different, the places they live are scattered around the globe, their specific actions varied, but they all end the same: large sums of money in the bank built up from little contributions. Most of these people never speak about their financial achievements because they don't want to stand out from their friends. Perhaps they assume their friends are doing the same. They view it as a wise and future-thinking act. Which, of course, it is.

Think of these folks in their retirement. I bet they do have a certain calm. They never have to worry that they will run out of money. These people can afford to go out to a nice dinner once in a while, or take in a show, or celebrate a special occasion by taking their entire family on a

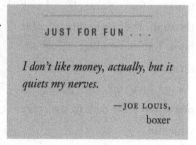

JUST FOR FUN . . .

I don't like money, actually, but it quiets my nerves.

—JOE LOUIS,
boxer

cruise. Their friends are never really sure how they can afford these luxuries.

Slow and steady.

Do you ever feel exhausted from trying to succeed? Are you so tired from planning your future that you have no energy to enjoy life today? Have you heard the old saying "Live in the moment"? Is that a joke for you because you are always checking the balance of your investment statements wondering if you are on track with your retirement plan or some other savings goal?

> *I know the price of success: dedication, hard work, and an unremitting devotion to the things you want to see happen.*
>
> —FRANK LLOYD WRIGHT, world-renowned architect

Listen to Solomon again. "Do not wear yourself out to get rich; have the wisdom to show restraint" (Proverbs 23:4). I hope you are convinced that nothing we are discussing is new. This wisdom has been around for thousands of years (Solomon lived three thousand years ago). We simply missed it or didn't believe it.

Believe in yourself. Believe you can achieve your dreams. Educate your children with words and by example. Believe, but don't cling. Work, but don't stress. Save, but don't rush.

As we approach the end of our lessons from King Solomon, I encourage you to continue on this path of wisdom. Don't take my word for it, but prove these truths for yourself. Look through the appendix of this book for more ideas. Read additional books on the subject. Never give up, but please do not allow your task to overtake your life.

> **A FINAL FUNNY . . .**
>
> *If at first you don't succeed, try, try again. Then quit. No use being a damn fool about it.*
>
> —W. C. FIELDS, entertainer

I included these "funny" comments throughout simply to suggest that we all need to relax a bit in our quest for financial freedom. Wisdom is found in the journey, not at the destination. Set your goals, dream your dreams, yet always bear in mind to enjoy the trip.

Remember, "a truth is true whether you believe in it or not."

We end where we began. In the introduction I stated, "If a lesson seems too simple, read it again. Sometimes the most life-changing truth comes dressed in simplicity." If you find it useful, read this book again.

I wish you happiness and wisdom in your life.

Questions to Ask Yourself

1. Since building wealth takes time, do I have the patience to stay the course?
2. Have I taken the time to realize the wealth I already have, especially compared to much of the rest of the world?
3. Do I view setbacks as opportunities in disguise? Do I allow setbacks to make me stronger?
4. Have I learned to enjoy the journey as well as the destination?
5. Am I developing financial patience?

Wisdom's To-Do List

1. Having goals for the future and being content in the present are not contradictory concepts. Take time to appreciate what you already have.

2. Thankfulness is a powerful component in happiness. What five things are you most thankful for?

3. The road to financial success has twists, steep grades, and surprises along the way. Slow and steady wins the race is more than a moral to a children's story. Determine to make progress, no matter how slight.

4. Get started.

ANCIENT ADVICE

PROVERBS 21:5—The plans of the diligent lead to profit as surely as haste leads to poverty.

PROVERBS 28:22—A stingy man is eager to get rich and is unaware that poverty awaits him.

PROVERBS 15:27—A greedy man brings trouble to his family, but he who hates bribes will live.

PROVERBS 28:20—A faithful man will be richly blessed, but one eager to get rich will not go unpunished.

PROVERBS 23:4–5—Do not wear yourself out to get rich; have the wisdom to show restraint. Cast but a glance at riches, and they are gone, for they will surely sprout wings and fly off to the sky like an eagle.

THE TEACHER

Abidan stopped midstride and watched a young man in the corner of the wide shop swing an adze. It was a warm day with little wind to cool Abidan's place of business. Abidan walked past the twenty other workers and stopped near the young man who was so intent on his work that he took no notice of his employer.

Leaning against his father's old workbench, Abidan studied the boy's movement. He recalled a time when his father had taught him to swing an adze.

"Yoshua." Abidan pulled on his gray beard. "You must slow down."

The boy jumped at the sound of Abidan's voice. "I am sorry, I did not hear you approach."

"I see that." Abidan rose and took the long handle of the adze and straddled the log resting on the floor. "Use shorter strokes, Yoshua. If you swing too hard and too fast, you will peel away more wood than is necessary." Abidan set the metal blade at the end of the adze on the log at the spot where Yoshua had been chopping, then brought the handle up and let it fall, directing the sharp metal edge under the bark but not into the

light wood. A section of bark chipped away. Abidan did it several times until he removed two cubits of bark.

"Come here, Yoshua. Look at the area I just cleared and the area you've been working. What do you see?"

"Yours is much smoother. I've cut into the tender wood."

"That is correct. The key is control and focus. New workers hold too high on the handle. For better control, move your hands closer to the blade and use smooth but short chops, taking away only the bark. Understand?"

"Yes. I understand. Shorter swings. Hold the handle lower."

"That is correct, at least for this task." Abidan handed the adze back to the boy. "Try again."

Yoshua took his position over the log and swung the adze the way Abidan had shown him.

"How does that feel? Do you have more control of the tool?"

"Yes. I should have known this."

Abidan laughed. "Don't be hard on yourself, Yoshua. All men learn from others and from experience. I learned from my father when I was just a boy. That was a long time ago, back when my father and I worked alone. So much has changed."

"You are the finest carpenter in the entire region. My father reminds me every day how fortunate I am to have found a trade with a willing teacher."

"Your father has asked that I teach you more than wood skills, Yoshua."

"My father has never told me how he knows you."

Abidan smiled. "I met him many years ago. He was still a baby in your grandmother's arms. I was just thirteen. Your grandmother's father was a faithful servant in King Solomon's court." He paused. "They taught me an important lesson about helping others."

"They taught you?"

"I first saw your grandmother on the street struggling to pick up a broken bundle of flax. She was holding the child who would become your father." Abidan leaned against his father's workbench and caressed one of the boards. Although it had been nearly thirty years since his father died, Abidan missed him terribly. He sighed, then drew his attention back to the present.

"I owe all I have to the lessons taught to me by King Solomon. I have promised to teach you those same lessons. I owe your family that much and more."

"You will share Solomon's lessons?"

Abidan nodded. *"Tell me, Yoshua, what does this saying mean? 'Finish your outdoor work and get your fields ready; after that, build your house'"* [Proverbs 24:27].

Yoshua looked at the floor and repeated the words . . .

APPENDIX

RECOMMENDED READING

George Samuel Clason, *The Richest Man in Babylon*. CreateSpace, 2008.

Bruce Fleet, *Demystifying Wall Street: Shedding a Little Light on the BULL!* AuthorHouse, 2007.

Benjamin Franklin, *Uncommon Cents: Secrets to Achieving Personal Financial Success*. Franklin Covey, 2004.

———*The Way to Wealth*. CreateSpace, 2008.

Michael M. Pompian, *Behavioral Finance and Wealth Management: How to Build Optimal Portfolios That Account for Investor Biases*. Wiley, 2006.

Steven K. Scott, *The Richest Man Who Ever Lived*. Doubleday Business, 2006.

Hersh Shefrin, *Beyond Greed and Fear: Understanding Behavioral Finance and the Psychology of Investing*. Oxford University Press, 2007.

Thomas J. Stanley, Ph.D., and William D. Danko, Ph.D., *The Millionaire Next Door*. Pocket, 1998.

Jason Zweig, *Your Money and Your Brain*. Simon & Schuster, 2008.

ADDITIONAL RESOURCES

Crown Financial Concepts: www.crownfinancialconcepts.com
My Spending Plan: www.myspendingplan.com
Quicken Online: www.quickenonline.com
The Bee Hive: www.thebeehive.org

ABOUT THE AUTHOR

Bruce Fleet is the founder and chairman of Fleet Capital Management, LLC, a fee-only investment management company in Colorado. A professional in the investment industry for more than two decades, he has received the Certified Investment Management Consultant (CIMA) designation and an Investment Strategist Certificate from the Wharton School of Business at the University of Pennsylvania, via the Investment Management Consultants Association.

Throughout his career, Fleet has been involved in teaching investors and professional investment advisers the fundamentals of proper and effective investment management. He is a frequently requested speaker, media guest, and industry trainer on investment management topics. Fleet founded and once chaired A Portion of My Heart, a ministries foundation. This foundation, based on Fleet's music, supported inner-city ministries throughout Denver, and provided support to World Vision internationally.

Fleet is also the author of *Demystifying Wall Street: Shedding a Little Light on the BULL!* He lives with his wife, Michelle, in a small town, high in the Colorado Rocky Mountains. His website can be found at www .brucefleet.com.

SHARE THE SECRETS OF SOLOMON!

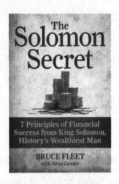

To order individual copies of the book:

Telephone Penguin Group (USA) Inc. Consumer Sales at 1-800-788-6262

Most Penguin Group books are available at special quantity discounts for bulk purchase for sales promotions, premiums, fund-raising, or educational use. Special books or book excerpts also can be created to fit specific needs.

Call PGI Special Markets for details on bulk quantity purchases. For *premiums, sales promotions, employee giveaways, fund-raisers,* or *reselling,* call 1-212-366-2612. Or write to Penguin Group (USA) Inc. Special Markets, 375 Hudson Street, New York, NY 10014.

Penguin's Business-to-Business Advantage program allows your local bookseller to offer special discounted pricing for bulk sales. Your business, school, nonprofit, or church can receive special discounted pricing, great service, direct shipping, and more. Call your local bookstore and say you'd like to use Penguin's B2B program to buy your books for giveaways or training.

The Solomon Secret • 978-1-58542-818-2 • $13.95 ($17.50 CAN)